T0274297

DECISIONS OF THE
VICKSBURG CAMPAIGN

OTHER BOOKS IN THE COMMAND DECISIONS IN AMERICA'S CIVIL WAR SERIES

Decisions at Stones River
Matt Spruill and Lee Spruill

Decisions at Second Manassas
Matt Spruill III and Matt Spruill IV

Decisions at Chickamauga
Dave Powell

Decisions at Chattanooga
Larry Peterson

Decisions of the Atlanta Campaign
Larry Peterson

Decisions of the 1862 Kentucky Campaign
Larry Peterson

Decisions at The Wilderness and Spotsylvania Court House
Dave Townsend

Decisions at Gettysburg, Second Edition
Matt Spruill

Decisions of the Tullahoma Campaign
Michael R. Bradley

Decisions at Antietam
Michael S. Lang

Decisions of the Seven Days
Matt Spruill

Decisions at Fredericksburg
Chris Mackowski

Decisions at Perryville
Larry Peterson

Decisions of the Maryland Campaign
Michael S. Lang

Decisions at Shiloh
Dave Powell

Decisions at Franklin
Andrew S. Bledsoe

Decisions of the 1862 Shenandoah Valley Campaign
Robert Tanner

Decisions at Kennesaw Mountain
Larry Peterson

DECISIONS
OF THE
VICKSBURG CAMPAIGN

The Eighteen Critical Decisions
That Defined the Operation

Larry Peterson

Maps by Matt Spruill

COMMAND DECISIONS
IN AMERICA'S CIVIL WAR
Matt Spruill and Larry Peterson,
Series Editors

The University of Tennessee Press / Knoxville

Copyright © 2024 by The University of Tennessee Press / Knoxville.
All Rights Reserved. Manufactured in the United States of America.
First Edition.

Library of Congress Cataloging-in-Publication Data

Names: Peterson, Lawrence K., author. | Spruill, Matt, cartographer.
Title: Decisions of the Vicksburg campaign : the eighteen critical decisions that
defined the operation / Larry Peterson ; maps by Matt Spruill.
Other titles: Command decisions in America's Civil War.
Description: First edition. | Knoxville : The University of Tennessee Press, [2024]
| Series: Command decisions in America's Civil War | Includes bibliographical
references and index. | Summary: "Vicksburg, nicknamed the Gibraltar of the
Confederacy, was vital to Confederate supply lines, troop movements, and access to
port cities on the Gulf of Mexico. The fortified city had been under constant attack
since 1862 as Admiral Farragut assaulted Vicksburg after capturing New Orleans,
and Major General Halleck enlisted then Major General Grant to devise an overland
campaign to support a naval engagement. As Vicksburg was heavily garrisoned and
resupplied regularly, Federal plans came up short again and again. But the pugnacious
Grant would eventually devise a bold plan to cross the Mississippi River and advance
along the western bank, use a feint by General Sherman's forces and a raid by Colonel
Grierson's cavalry to draw out Confederate troops, then recross the river and capture
Vicksburg. *Decisions of the Vicksburg Campaign* explores the critical decisions made
by Confederate and Federal commanders during the battle and how these decisions
shaped its outcome. Complete with maps and a driving tour, this volume is nineteenth
in the Command Decisions in America's Civil War series"—Provided by publisher.
Identifiers: LCCN 2024016793 (print) | LCCN 2024016794 (ebook) |
ISBN 9781621908609 (paperback) | ISBN 9781621908746 (pdf) |
ISBN 9781621909101 (kindle edition)
Subjects: LCSH: Command of troops—Case studies. | Vicksburg (Miss.)—
History—Civil War, 1861–1865. | Vicksburg (Miss.)—History—Siege, 1863. |
United States—History—Civil War, 1861–1865—Campaigns.
Classification: LCC E475.2 .P47 2024 (print) | LCC E475.2 (ebook) |
DDC 973.7/344—dc23/eng/20240430
LC record available at https://lccn.loc.gov/2024016793
LC ebook record available at https://lccn.loc.gov/2024016794

To the soldiers and sailors on both sides
who fought for what they believed.

CONTENTS

ILLUSTRATIONS

Figures

Maps

PREFACE

My first connection and introduction to Vicksburg and the Vicksburg Campaign occurred in 1968. While a new US Air Force second lieutenant in training to become a communications officer, I was temporarily based at Keesler Air Force Base in Biloxi, Mississippi. One weekend, I visited Vicksburg National Military Park with my new wife, Kathleen. As we were driving along the tour route, we saw a marker mentioning a General Vaughn. I had grown up knowing that one of my great-great-grandfathers was Confederate brigadier general Alfred J. Vaughan, so we assumed that he had participated in the siege. That turned out to be incorrect! Interestingly, out of 428 Confederate general officers, 2 had the last name of Vaugh(a)n. The other one was Brig. Gen. John C. Vaughn, who indeed was at Vicksburg during the siege. This officer later gained some slight fame as part of the escort accompanying Confederate president Jefferson Davis from the time he fled the rebel capital of Richmond until his capture by Union cavalry at Irwinville, Georgia.

From an early age I became fascinated with history, and especially that of the Civil War. I enjoyed several television series about that conflict and read some books concerning it. However, it wasn't until late in my flying career that I decided to learn more about Brig. Gen. Alfred J. Vaughan. Hampered by the fact that there were two Vaugh(a)ns who were Confederate generals, I began to read about the battles and events my ancestor participated in, and I started traveling to the many battlefields and sites where he served as a commander in the Confederate Armies of the Mississippi and Tennessee. I also spent a lot of time conducting research in state libraries. After some eighteen years of work, during which I used an amazing amount of information published by Vaughan's grandson Jack C. Vaughan, I saw my book *Confederate Combat Commander: The Remarkable Life of Brigadier General Alfred Jefferson Vaughan Jr.* published in 2013 by the University of Tennessee Press.

During my research travels I discovered and joined the Rocky Mountain Civil War Round Table, based in the Denver area. There I met historian and author Matt Spruill, who assisted me in polishing my Vaughan manuscript and getting it before the University of Tennessee Press. Matt then asked me to be a coeditor with him for a proposed new series concerning the critical decisions of Civil War campaigns and battles. Thus, here I am—with several books in that series already published, and more, including this one, to come! Working daily with Matt to review the many other works in the Command Decisions in America's Civil War series has certainly rounded out my grasp of Civil War history. Due to my ancestor general I have become a serious student of the less appreciated operations within the Western Theater.

The Vicksburg Campaign stands out as perhaps the finest example of a military campaign during the entire Civil War. Although it took a while to get underway in any meaningful fashion, once Maj. Gen. Ulysses S. Grant landed on the eastern shore of the Mississippi below Vicksburg, the offensive really took off, and it makes for fascinating reading. Instead of focusing on the day-to-day events that took place, this book, like all others in the series, will examine how eighteen critical decisions formed the outcome of the campaign. Rather than seeing what happened during the fighting, we will observe why the fighting happened the way it did.

My definition of a critical decision is that it is one that helped to determine the outcome of the campaign from that point on. All of our authors encountered the problem of separating these few critical decisions from the many others. In any army on a given day, thousands of decisions are made by commanders at all levels. Most of these are basic, based on higher-level choices. Some of these are important decisions, but very few are critical. A decision hierarchy might look something like this:

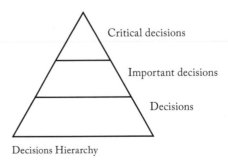

Decisions Hierarchy

There are six categories of critical decisions: tactical, strategic, organizational, operational, logistical, and personnel. Typically these decisions are made by commanders at the higher levels, but that is not always true. Often critical decisions made before the campaign or battle profoundly influence the outcome. While some of these choices are obvious, others can be subtle. The reader may use this framework to examine any Civil War battle or campaign, as well as those of other wars.

Our successful format for analyzing each critical decision begins with a discussion of the situation the decision-maker faced. Evaluation of the options available is next, followed by examination of the option chosen, which is the critical decision. The results and impact of the choice are then presented, along with the long-term effect on the campaign or battle. Occasionally, to the dismay of some, we present an alternate scenario: What if the decision-maker had chosen a different option? This allows the reader to speculate how the outcome of the fighting might have significantly changed.

I have divided the Vicksburg Campaign into the following time frames, with a chapter devoted to each. The critical decisions each chapter are listed below:

There are a few items to note while reading this work. First, the abbreviations of Union (and sometimes Confederate) corps were not indicated via roman numerals until long after the Civil War: view the US War Department's *War of the Rebellion: A Compilation of the Official Records of the Union and Confederate Armies* (hereafter referred to as *Official Records*) for proof. Therefore, I don't use roman numerals, except in some maps where space is at a premium. Furthermore, this book uses the abbreviations for military ranks employed during the Civil War, not those currently in use. Also, time and time zones were not standardized until 1883, so times of day indicated in the book may be incorrect, depending on what the person involved was using as his standard.

ACKNOWLEDGMENTS

Special thanks to Dr. Timothy Smith for his help with this work. Thanks to Vicksburg historians Edwin C. Bearss, Terrance Winschel, Michael Ballard, and Parker Hills, whose prolific research and documentation made my grasp of the campaign easier. I appreciated the loan of Ed Bearss's trilogy by fellow officer Don Hallstrom of the Rocky Mountain Civil War Round Table.

Due to the tireless efforts of the American Battlefield Trust, sites relevant to the Vicksburg Campaign have been preserved and will continue to be, thereby saving this legacy for present and future generations. Hats off to past trust president James Lighthizer and current president David Duncan and their staffs for their unrelenting efforts in saving Vicksburg Campaign ground.

I am so blessed to continue to work with the exceptional staff of the University of Tennessee Press, including my editor Thomas Wells, Jon Boggs, Stephanie Thompson, and Walt Evans. Special thanks to our series copyeditor Elizabeth Crowder for once again making my manuscript so much more readable.

Thanks also to coeditor Matt Spruill for his continued friendship and expertise in fine-tuning the manuscript, as well as providing the maps!

Finally, thanks to my longtime wife and partner, Kathleen, for supporting me on yet another attempt to describe a Civil War campaign, as well as for keeping my computer under control!

INTRODUCTION

The Civil War formally began with the shelling of Union-controlled Fort Sumter, located in South Carolina's Charleston Harbor, in the heart of the newly established Confederacy, on April 12, 1861. But the war was years in the making. While its cause is a completely separate subject with its own set of literature, we will simplify it to the question of whether slavery should remain legal in the United States. Southern leaders tied this issue to states' rights. After numerous attempts over many years to mollify both the Northern and Southern sides, the opponents finally came to blows. Seven Southern states seceded from the United States by early 1861, meeting in Montgomery, Alabama, to form the Confederate States of America. Fort Sumter endured some thirty-four hours of bombardment before its commanding officer, Maj. Robert Anderson, surrendered.[1]

President Abraham Lincoln immediately called for seventy-five thousand volunteers for ninety days' military service. Southern men scrambled to enlist to protect their homeland. Few suspected that the war would last more than a short period; they were soon proved wrong.[2]

Geographically, the Civil War devolved into three theaters: Eastern, Western, and Trans-Mississippi. I will briefly examine the major actions in each to bring the reader up to date about events before the Vicksburg Campaign began. In the Eastern Theater, it was all about pressing "on to Richmond." The city was the final capital of the Confederacy, now numbering eleven Southern states and potentially several border states as well. Both sides were ill prepared for any combat; there was no uniformity of uniforms and flags, and military accouterments were in short supply. Unaware of the complexities of establishing and training an army, new Union commander in chief Abraham Lincoln soon ordered field commander Maj. Gen. Irvin McDowell to attack the Confederate army south of Washington, DC. McDowell unwillingly led his command into contact with the Confederates at Bull Run near Manassas, Virginia, some twenty miles or so southwest of the Union capital. On July 21, the First Battle of Bull Run, or the Battle of First Manassas, began with Federal success. But with reinforcements received just in time, the Confederates turned the tide, sending their enemy fleeing back into the District of Columbia. Little-known Brig. Gen. Thomas J. Jackson, a former instructor at the Virginia Military Institute, helped hold the Confederate battle line and received the nickname "Stonewall" for his action. Both sides quickly realized that proper training, standardized flags and uniforms, and requisite supplies had to be provided before significant further combat would be successful. Thus, little important action took place during the rest of 1861 in this theater.[3]

Lincoln recognized that his general-in-chief Maj. Gen. Winfield Scott was entirely too old and feeble to command his eastern army. Therefore, the president appointed Maj. Gen. George B. McClellan to that command. A superb organizer, McClellan soon constructed the Army of the Potomac into a large, well-armed, well-trained force. However, he would soon prove to be too cautious to use its combat power.[4]

In 1862 "Little Mac," as McClellan was nicknamed, presented the president with an elaborate plan to capture the Confederate capital at Richmond. The general would send his huge army of some one hundred thousand soldiers by ship to Fort Monroe, located at the tip of the peninsula between the York and James Rivers in eastern Virginia. From there, the army would advance on land to the Confederate capital, capture it, and end the war. Little Mac quickly demonstrated extreme cautiousness in leading the campaign, but he eventually moved his army to within hearing range of Richmond's church bells. When McClellan was finally attacked by Confederate commander Gen. Joseph E. Johnston at the Battle of Seven Pines, or Fair Oaks, a complete change of action occurred. After Johnston was wounded during that battle, Pres. Jefferson Davis replaced him with Gen. Robert E. Lee, presently his military adviser. Lee had been largely unsuccessful so far, but in one of the more spectacular turnarounds of military success, he commenced waging the Seven Days Battles in late June. This fighting ultimately sent the Army of the Potomac reeling back to Washington, DC.[5]

Encouraged by his success, Lee advanced. With the help of his subordinate Maj. Gen. Thomas "Stonewall" Jackson (whose nickname referred to his stand at First Manassas, or Bull Run), Lee successfully corralled and defeated a new Union army commanded by Maj. Gen. John Pope at the Battle of Second Manassas, also called the Second Battle of Bull Run. Emboldened by his success, Lee decided to advance into Maryland, taking the war into Yankee territory. Part of his command captured Harpers Ferry, Virginia (later West Virginia), but McClellan moved his Army of the Potomac to block the Confederate advance. On September 17, 1862, the two armies fought the Battle of Antietam along Antietam Creek near Sharpsburg, Maryland. During this bloodiest single day of the entire Civil War, Lee's soldiers managed to hold off the Yankees. However, confronted by a larger force, Lee discovered that he had no choice but to retreat into Virginia, ending the Maryland Campaign.[6]

Disturbed by McClellan's failure to pursue Lee aggressively back into Virginia, Lincoln replaced him with Maj. Gen. John Pope. Pope attempted to skirt around Lee near Fredericksburg, Virginia, but the arrival of pontoons necessary to cross the Rappahannock River was delayed. When he could finally use the pontoons to cross, on December 13 Pope ordered assaults against Lee's well-entrenched army. The result was thirteen thousand Federal casualties versus fewer than half that many Confederate ones. An abortive "Mud March" quickly ended Pope's short command of the Army of the Potomac.[7]

President Lincoln replaced Pope with the pompous Maj. Gen. Joseph Hooker. Hooker worked hard to rebuild the army, and he devised a plan to maneuver around Lee's army positioned to protect Richmond. In early May 1863, the Union commander initially was successful in turning Lee's position and forcing him to quickly regroup. However, Hooker almost immediately lost his initiative. Stonewall Jackson suggested a turning movement to outflank Hooker's Eleventh Corps, which was largely left unprotected near Chancellorsville. Jackson proceeded to conduct the movement on May 2, unbeknownst to the Federals. In perhaps Lee's finest battle, this turning movement rolled up the Eleventh Corps, ultimately providing a significant rebel victory and forcing Hooker to retreat. Unfortunately for the Confederacy, some of Jackson's own troops wounded him later that evening while performing a reconnaissance in the dark. On May 10, he died from pneumonia, leaving Lee without his finest corps commander. Jackson's death perhaps indirectly contributed to Confederate failure in the upcoming battle.[8]

Undoubtedly emboldened by his success at Chancellorsville, Robert E. Lee convinced the Confederate high command to condone an invasion of Pennsylvania. Possibly to assist in gaining foreign recognition (although this was unlikely, because President Lincoln had issued the Emancipation Proclamation effective January 1, 1863) and to spare the Virginia farmers, Lee would invade Pennsylvania with his army. This he proceeded to do, with some troops advancing as far as York and Carlisle. Meanwhile, Hooker abruptly resigned. Lincoln appointed the competent but testy Maj. Gen. George G. Meade to command, even as the Confederate Army of Northern Virginia was maneuvering in Pennsylvania. Meade knew he had to protect Washington, DC, and Baltimore from enemy raiding. This set the stage for the largest battle of the war.[9]

By late June Lee's army had marched well into Pennsylvania, pursued by Meade's army. Due to Maj. Gen. James "Jeb" Stuart's cavalry riding around the Union troops, the Confederate commander had little knowledge about the location of his foe, and he reassembled his various commands at the small town of Gettysburg on July 1. An advance Union cavalry force commanded by Brig. Gen. John Buford delayed the Confederates' progress through the town, allowing the arriving Federal corps to dig in on the high ground south and east of it. The next day, Lee ordered an assault on what he believed to be the end of the Union line, but that line had in fact been extended. Late-afternoon assaults at the Peach Orchard and Devil's Den ultimately failed. On July 3 Lee ordered another assault on Culp's Hill, which also failed, and then the infamous Pickett-Pettigrew-Trimble charge. After waiting a day after the unsuccessful events of the third, he ordered a retreat that brought his army back into Virginia. This was the biggest battle of the war, casualties on both sides totaled some fifty thousand. For the Union, the victory at Gettysburg coincided with the successful end to the Vicksburg Campaign, the subject of this book, as well as the Tullahoma Campaign, which gained most of Tennessee for the Federals.[10]

In the Trans-Mississippi Theater several actions of note had taken place. The state of Missouri was divided in terms of loyalties, with both sides coveting control of it. Although skirmishing and maneuvering began with the war's start, the first real battle took place in August 1861 at Wilson's Creek, in the southern part of Missouri near Springfield. This fighting was initiated by Union commander Brig. Gen. Nathaniel Lyon, whose smaller force assaulted a Confederate army from Arkansas. This rebel force was commanded by Brig. Gen. Ben McColloch and assisted by Missouri troops led by former governor Sterling Price. Initially successful, the Union force was eventually defeated and its commander killed, giving the Confederates a victory.[11]

On March 7, 1862, a Confederate army commanded by Maj. Gen. Earl Van Dorn attacked what he believed was the rear of a small Union army commanded by Brig. Gen. Samuel R. Curtis. Much to Van Dorn's surprise, Curtis realigned his command and confronted the Confederates at the Battle of Pea Ridge in Arkansas. The following day Van Dorn's men were routed by a Federal charge, giving the Yankees a victory.[12]

Later in March, a small Union force from Fort Union first held back part of a Rebel army commanded by Brig. Gen. Henry H. Sibley that was attempting to secure the New Mexico Territory for the Confederacy. While confronted at Glorieta Pass east of Santa Fe, part of the Union command led by Maj. John Chivington (later of Sand Creek Massacre fame) maneuvered behind the invaders' lines and destroyed their supplies, including rations. This ended Confederate efforts to maintain control of this western territory, potentially all the way to California, forcing an exhausting retreat back to Texas.[13]

On December 7, another small battle took place at Prairie Grove, Arkansas, where a command largely made up of Confederate conscripts led by Maj. Gen. Thomas Hindman attacked several divisions of Union soldiers. Rebuffed, Hindman's command melted away.[14]

The Trans-Mississippi Theater supplied the Confederacy with necessities such as cattle, and it harbored some fairly large armies. Much of the time, these Confederate soldiers rendered little to the theater while they could have been better used elsewhere. After the Vicksburg Campaign successfully opened the Mississippi River to Union traffic and blocked trade from it, the Trans-Mississippi Theater ceased to be much of a factor for the rest of the war.[15]

The Western Theater was comparatively much larger than the Eastern Theater. Action in the Eastern Theater mostly took place in the one hundred or so miles between the two capitals of Richmond and Washington, and little change occurred there during most of the war other than the killing and wounding of many thousands of soldiers on both sides. However, almost from the beginning of the Civil War, the Union armies assigned to the Western Theater generally made continuous progress in capturing Confederate territory within it. Infighting in the main Confederate army assigned to protect this theater, the Army of Tennessee, only made defense of its territory that much more difficult. Covering the states west of the Allegheny Mountains, south of the Ohio River, and east of the Mississippi River, the Western Theater encompassed immense distances for maneuvering. Often limited by weather to rivers and railroads, supply lines were long and vulnerable to being severed. The Vicksburg Campaign, orchestrated by Maj. Gen. Ulysses S. Grant, was conducted in this theater.[16]

At the beginning of the war, while Pres. Jefferson Davis waited for Gen. Albert S. Johnston, soon to be a general, to take command of this huge theater, others created a Confederate line of defense stretching some four

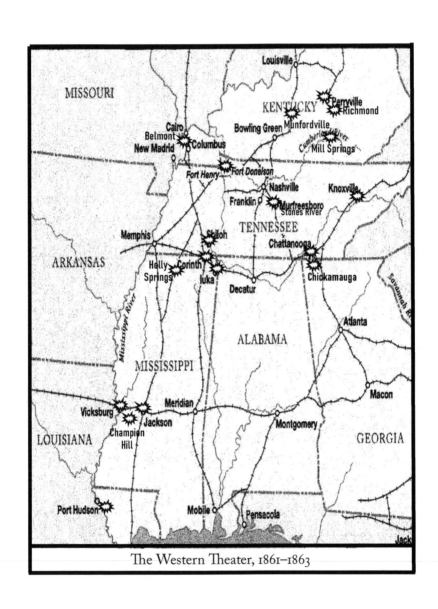

The Western Theater, 1861–1863

hundred miles west from Cumberland Gap to the Mississippi River. That river provided a vital path through the Confederacy for Union craft, which needed to be prevented from using it. In fact, at the beginning of the war general-in-chief Winfield Scott proposed his "Anaconda Plan," which involved capturing the entire Mississippi River and establishing a blockade along the Atlantic Ocean and Gulf of Mexico shores.[17]

Temporarily commanding much of the Western Theater was Davis's old friend from his West Point days, Maj. Gen. Leonidas Polk, bishop of Louisiana. With no military experience since he left West Point, and now serving in this extremely important position, Polk cast his eye on the only high ground along the Mississippi River between Cairo, Illinois, and Memphis, Tennessee. Located at Columbus, Kentucky, it was the perfect place for a large battery of cannon to prohibit Union traffic from sailing downriver. At the beginning of the war, the Commonwealth of Kentucky had declared itself neutral, allowing no military movements within its boundaries. Although both sides built up military forces within the commonwealth, they were very careful to pretend not to violate this impartiality. Nonetheless, the bishop-general decided that he needed Columbus to protect the Mississippi River (including his plantation in Mississippi, located nearby). On September 4, 1861, Polk ordered his troops to capture Columbus, violating the neutrality of Kentucky. He immediately established a series of batteries to guard the river.[18]

Within the Union high command in the Western Theater was a relatively unknown brigadier general named Ulysses S. Grant. A graduate of West Point and a veteran of the Mexican-American War, Grant had been stationed on the West Coast, apart from his family, and he had resigned due to excessive drinking after being warned by his commander. After failing at several civilian pursuits, he sought and received command of an Illinois regiment with the advent of the Civil War. Soon after, he received his commission as a brigadier. Grant would make his mark first in this theater before eventually taking command of all Union armies.[19]

Quickly responding to Polk's invasion of Kentucky, Grant moved to and captured Paducah, located at the mouth of the Tennessee River. Later, on November 7, he took a small command down the Mississippi and off-loaded his troops just north of the tiny town of Belmont, Missouri, which was directly across the river from Columbus. He then marched his men to that town, where a small Confederate camp was located. Polk, observing the Yankees, sent several regiments across the river to confront Grant. Fighting broke out, with the Union soldiers eventually forcing the Confederates out of their encampment. However, the victorious Federals then stopped to loot the camp. Realizing the Confederate disaster unfolding, Polk bombarded the site and sent additional troops to repel the Yankees. This forced Grant to retreat, which he managed to do successfully. Both sides suffered about six hundred casualties each. Sam Grant had conducted his first offensive operation.[20]

To commanders on both sides, three rivers stood out as obvious paths into the Confederate interior, or heartland. The Mississippi has already been briefly discussed. The Tennessee River flowed southwest from near Knoxville, Tennessee, almost to Corinth, Mississippi, before turning north to empty into the Ohio River at Paducah. The Cumberland River flowed west to northwest, passing the Tennessee state capital of Nashville before emptying into the Ohio River just east of Paducah, at Smithland. Guarding these rivers were two Confederate forts located just upriver from their mouths in Tennessee. Fort Henry protected the Tennessee River, although engineers located it in a floodplain. Construction of better-located Fort Heiman, above and across the river, had just started. Confederate engineers positioned Fort Donelson on much better ground to halt any Union gunboats trying to sail up the Cumberland. The two forts were only a dozen miles apart.[21]

The first break in the long Confederate line occurred when Brig. Gen. George H. Thomas defeated a small Union command at the Battle of Mill Springs, or Logan's Cross Roads, on January 19, 1862, in south central Kentucky. Observing the obvious opportunity, Grant petitioned to advance with the help of the "brown water" navy to capture Fort Henry. Finally receiving permission, he easily captured the stronghold on February 6, then marched his command to Fort Donelson without clearance. The guns there stopped the navy's advance, disabling most of the gunboats. After several days of fighting, the Confederate garrison surrendered "unconditionally" to Grant.[22]

Based on this success, the next Union movement was upstream on the Tennessee to a high, dry location at Pittsburg Landing. Under orders, Grant waited here for the arrival of the Army of the Ohio, which would join his force and advance to the very important military target of Corinth, the junction of the east–west Memphis and Charleston Railroad and the north–south Mobile and Ohio Railroad. General Johnston scrambled to combine several different commands to advance to the landing and attack Grant before he could be reinforced. Due to confusion, the new Confederate Army of the Mississippi attacked on April 6, later than Johnston originally planned. Nonetheless, the rebels surprised the Yankees at the landing, with the small Shiloh Church nearby. Due to further confusion on the battlefield, especially because of its diverse terrain, the Confederates became disorganized. But they almost succeeded in driving the Union command present into the Tennessee River. However, the untimely death of General Johnston, the highest-ranking general killed on either side during the Civil War, along with the decision to wait until the following day to complete the victory, gave Grant the time he needed to reorganize. Reinforced by the timely arrival of the Army of the Ohio, the next day the Union commander took the offensive and defeated the tired and hungry members of the Army of the Mississippi. The Battle of Shiloh, the bloodiest day of the war so far, gave the Union a solid, if costly, victory.[23]

Following the Battle of Shiloh, Maj. Gen. Henry W. Halleck, commander of the enlarged Department of the Mississippi, increased his army with other commands until he then had some 120,000 soldiers. Placing Grant in the meaningless position of second-in-command, he advanced toward Corinth at an excruciatingly slow rate, almost causing Grant to resign. Thankfully for the Union, Grant's friend Maj. Gen. William T. Sherman convinced him to remain in the army. After the Confederates abandoned Corinth in the face of the overwhelming Union force, they fled to Tupelo.[24]

After the capture of Corinth Halleck split up his huge command, failing to take advantage of its strength. Fearing the hot, inclement summer weather in the state of Mississippi, he decided against moving to and capturing Vicksburg, eventually, as we will see, leaving that feat to Grant. Halleck sent part of his command toward Chattanooga, but it was turned by Gen. Braxton Bragg's futile Kentucky Campaign. U. S. Grant, then commanding a district of southern Tennessee and northeastern Mississippi, was somewhat involved in directing battles at Iuka in September and Corinth in October. Halleck was subsequently called to Washington, DC, as general in chief, a position in which he acted more as chief clerk. After his departure, Grant was elevated to department command, at which point we take up the Vicksburg Campaign.[25]

CHAPTER 1

BEFORE THE VICKSBURG
CAMPAIGN BEGINS
SEPTEMBER 30–OCTOBER 25, 1862

If you have bypassed the preface, please direct your attention there and read the definition of a critical decision in order to understand the discussions more fully in this book.

Two critical decisions, both concerning personnel, preceded the Vicksburg Campaign. The US and Confederate presidents each made one, eventually pitting a strong field commander against a weak one. Also an organizational critical decision made by Pres. Jefferson Davis failed to unify command of the Mississippi River.

Davis Appoints Pemberton Commander of the Department of Mississippi and Eastern Louisiana

Situation

Named for Newitt Vick, a Methodist preacher who arrived in the area in 1809, Vicksburg and the surrounding high bluffs provided an excellent location for a town. With its abundance of walnut trees, this area came to be

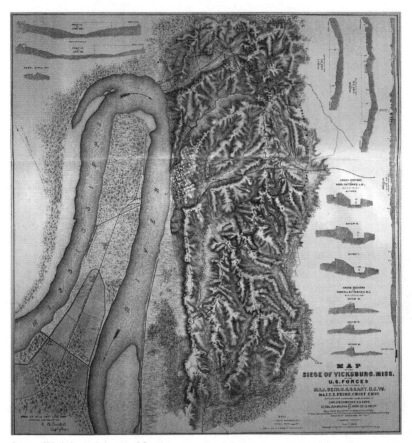

Siege of Vicksburg. Library of Congress.

known as the Walnut Hills, a name given to it by passing boatmen. The land was originally a cotton plantation established around 1800 and first owned by one Elihu H. Bay. A kinsman of his named Robert Turnbull continued to grow cotton. Around the edges of this property Vick began making lots available for sale in 1819. Although he died before the town was incorporated in 1825, Vick's descendants lobbied to name it in his honor. Mississippi became the twentieth US state in 1817.[1]

Vicksburg, commanding the Mississippi with its elevation above the river and that river's hairpin turn in passing the town, was an extremely important military stronghold because of its potential to halt Union passage past its heavily fortified batteries. While not impregnable by Federal warcraft and other vessels (Rear Adm. David G. Farragut managed to pass the Vicksburg batteries heading upstream on June 28, 1862), as of April 1863, some thirty-seven large-caliber cannon and thirteen fieldpieces lined the eastern shore of the Mississippi. By this time the armed city was the last main obstruction to Union passage down the river.[2]

Both Vicksburg and Port Hudson, located to the city's south and some 27 river miles north of Louisiana's capital of Baton Rouge and 240 river miles south of Vicksburg, had long been the focus for Union capture. Part of Maj. Gen. Winfield Scott's Anaconda Plan for defeating the newly established Confederate States of America entailed freeing the Mississippi River from Confederate control. The capture of Fort Pillow and Memphis to the north, and New Orleans and Baton Rouge to the south, left this stretch of the river as the final Union target. Meanwhile, shipments of grain and cattle had to move east along the Ohio River, and similar supplies headed to the Confederate interior were allowed to pass across the Mississippi from Texas, part of Louisiana, and other sources to the west.[3]

After his capture of Corinth following the Battle of Shiloh, Maj. Gen. Henry W. Halleck had the opportunity to move directly to Vicksburg and potentially capture the town. However, partly due to the excessively hot and humid summer climate there, he split up his massive army and directed various parts to other objectives, in particular Chattanooga. Thus Halleck lost the opportunity to advance rapidly to capture Vicksburg, roughly two hundred miles southwest of Corinth, by late spring or early summer 1862.[4]

Maj. Gen. Ulysses S. Grant, commanding the Union Department and Army of West Tennessee, a remnant of Halleck's former large force, received orders on August 2 from Halleck: "It is very desirable that you should clear out West Tennessee and North Mississippi of all organized enemies." Grant then ordered Maj. Gens. William S. Rosecrans and Edward O. C. Ord to capture Maj. Gen. Sterling Price's small Confederate army located near Iuka, Mississippi. A joint attack formulated by Grant himself failed to capture Price on September 19; Ord never joined the assault, as he was apparently unable to hear the battle initiated by Rosecrans. Price managed to escape and finally joined up with Maj. Gen. Earl Van Dorn's small army. As the senior officer, Van Dorn then advanced these two small armies toward Corinth, Mississippi, in an attempt to recover this important railroad crossing for the Confederacy. On October 3 and 4 he unsuccessfully assaulted the Corinth defenses manned by Rosecrans's army. While a disgusted Maj. Gen. Ulysses S. Grant watched, Van Dorn managed to escape almost certain defeat at the Davis Bridge, which allowed crossing of the Hatchie River. Rosecrans failed to actively pursue the Confederate commander.[5]

President Jefferson Davis, CSA.
*The Photographic History of the
Civil War*, Vol. X, p. 289.

When Van Dorn failed to capture Corinth on October 3–4, 1862, Pres. Jefferson Davis, in his active role as commander in chief of the Confederate armies, realized that he needed to address the situation out west. He needed a commander who could actively defend the Mississippi valley from Union incursion. As noted, Van Dorn had assumed overall command over Maj. Gen. Sterling Price's equally small army, and he had failed to defeat Maj. Gen. William S. Rosecrans's small army at Corinth. As far as Davis was concerned, Van Dorn no longer satisfied the requirements for his role.[6]

Options

President Davis had made up his mind to appoint a new commander for the Department of Mississippi and East Louisiana (that part of Louisiana east of the Mississippi River). Whom did he deem available and suited for that position? Apparently, Davis had the choice of three different general officers. The first man Davis considered was Maj. Gen. John C. Pemberton, commander of the Department of South Carolina, Georgia, and Florida. Other officers he could contemplate appointing were Gen. Joseph E. Johnston, who had recovered from his wounds during the Battle of Seven Pines (or Fair Oaks), or perhaps Gen. P. G. T. Beauregard, hero of the Battle of First Manassas, or Bull Run.[7]

Lieut. John C. Pemberton,
CSA. *The Photographic History
of the Civil War*, Vol. X, p. 249.

Option 1

Pemberton was a native of Pennsylvania and an 1837 graduate of the United States Military Academy. During the Mexican-American War he won two brevets for gallantry. His marriage to Martha Thompson of Norfolk, Virginia, in 1848 shifted his loyalty to the Confederacy. Pemberton resigned from the US Army on April 24, 1861. He was soon assigned to the Department of South Carolina, Georgia, and Florida under the command of Gen. Robert E. Lee, and he was promoted to brigadier general on June 17, 1861. When Lee was recalled to Richmond, Pemberton replaced him as commander of that department and was promoted to major general on January 14, 1862.[8]

Unfortunately, Pemberton could not relate to the South Carolina politicians within his department as well as Lee had. However, Jefferson Davis was greatly annoyed at Pemberton's mistreatment by these individuals.[9]

Option 2

Gen. Joe Johnston had more or less recovered from his wounding at the Battle of Seven Pines (Fair Oaks) on May 31, 1862. He had incurred Davis's wrath for complaining about his ranking as other than the most senior Confederate general. Johnston, who had been a staff brigadier general in the US Army, believed he outranked the president's other appointees to the rank of general, but Jefferson Davis considered line-officer ranks ahead of staff ranks.

The president could logically send Johnston west to command this important district, and this would put physical distance between the two disputants.[10]

<u>Option 3</u>

Beauregard had also incurred Davis's wrath. After the Creole general had directed the first major victory of the war at First Manassas (Bull Run), the president sent him west to aid Gen. Albert S. Johnston as he prepared for what became the Battle of Shiloh. Upon Johnston's death on the first day of fighting, Beauregard assumed command, but he halted the fighting with Confederate victory almost complete. Grant, reinforced with Maj. Gen. Don Carlos Buell's Army of the Ohio, clinched victory the following day, driving the Confederates back to Corinth. At this point Beauregard took unauthorized sick leave from the army, and Davis took advantage of his absence by relieving him of command. Beauregard's status was in limbo, but the president was loath to place him in a truly important command.[11]

Some readers might wonder whether Maj. Gen. Edmund Kirby Smith could have been an option for leading the Department of Mississippi and East Louisiana. They should remember that he was in Kentucky, winning the Battle of Richmond on August 30. He would soon be prepared to meet the enemy, as Bragg successfully fought the Battle of Perryville on October 8.[12]

Decision

As previously mentioned, Jefferson Davis was angered by Pemberton's treatment by the South Carolina politicians. Therefore, he decided to remove Pemberton from the Department of South Carolina, Georgia, and Florida and send him west to command the Department of Mississippi and East Louisiana. Davis issued orders for the command change on September 30, 1862.[13]

Results/Impact

The new commander of the Department of Mississippi and East Louisiana was tasked in particular with defending the Mississippi River from Vicksburg south to Port Hudson. These locations were the last two bastions protecting the river from Union incursion. However, Pemberton quickly realized that he was junior to both Van Dorn and Maj. Gen. Mansfield Lovell, formerly in command of the city of New Orleans. In order to clarify the command situation, Davis had Pemberton promoted to lieutenant general, to rank from October 10, 1862. Never experienced in combat operations, Pemberton would quickly demonstrate a lack of combat skills and maneuverability. Under his authority both Vicksburg and Port Hudson would fall to Union commanders the following July, opening the Mississippi River to total Federal control. Pemberton's failure to protect and defend Vicksburg significantly degraded the Confederacy's ability to resist further advances into the heart of the new nation. Interestingly, Gen. P. G. T. Beauregard replaced Pemberton as commander of the Department of South Carolina, Georgia, and Florida.[14]

Alternate Scenario

How different might the Vicksburg Campaign have been had anyone besides John Pemberton, bereft of combat experience, been selected for that command? If given a defined command, Johnston, a defensive general, might have more aggressively defended the city and bastion. Could he potentially have held off Grant for a longer period of time? A very interesting consideration![15]

Stanton Appoints Grant to Command
the Department of the Tennessee

Situation

Corinth had already been abandoned by the Confederates. Even so, after Halleck's successful capture of that city on May 30, 1862, the Union commander divided his massive army of some 120,000 soldiers and sent them to different objectives. He ordered Buell and his Army of the Ohio to advance toward Chattanooga, a vital Confederate railroad junction. Halleck discarded the opportunity to move on Vicksburg. As for Grant, disgusted with his lack of a command, since Halleck had appointed him to the meaningless position of second-in-command of his army, the former resident of Galena, Illinois, then obtained permission to leave the department. However, most fortuitously for the Union cause, Maj. Gen. William T. Sherman, Sam Grant's longtime close friend, advised him to remain in the army. Grant petitioned Halleck to remove himself to Memphis to command that district, and his request was granted.[16]

On July 11 a major organizational change for the Union armies occurred. Halleck was appointed general-in-chief and tasked with commanding all of the armies in order to better manage them. He departed for Washington, DC. This left Grant effectively in charge of the Department of the Tennessee without, however, being officially placed in command. Nonetheless, he conducted operations against Confederates within the department, including the Iuka affair and Battle of Corinth described above. Grant continued to do his best to operate successfully within his district.[17]

General in Chief Maj. Gen.
Henry W. Halleck, USA. *The
Photographic History of the Civil
War*, Vol. X, p. 165.

Options

Eventually Halleck realized that he needed to formally appoint a commander
for the Department of the Tennessee, since he was no longer present to command it himself. He logically should have considered the current commander
of the District of West Tennessee, Grant, as one option. However, another
general officer, Maj. Gen. John A. McClernand, was politicking heavily for
the position.[18]

Option 1

The present commander of the District of West Tennessee, U. S. Grant, was
born in 1822, and he graduated from West Point in the class of 1843. Assigned
to the infantry, he was twice breveted in the Mexican-American War. Unfortunately, while stationed in the Pacific Northwest and separated from his
family, Sam Grant apparently took to alcohol and, after a warning from his
commanding officer, resigned as of July 31, 1854. For the next six years, until
the beginning of the Civil War, Grant tried and failed to work as a farmer,
real estate salesman, candidate for county engineer, and customhouse clerk.
By 1861 he was clerking for his father and brothers' leather store in Galena,
Illinois.

At the beginning of the Civil War, with the assistance of his congress-
man Elihu B. Washburne, the governor of Illinois appointed Grant colonel of the Twenty-First Illinois Infantry. From that point on, Grant's mil-

Maj. Gen. Ulysses S. Grant,
USA . *The Photographic History
of the Civil War*, Vol. X, p. 39.

itary career swiftly advanced. He was engaged in a small fight at Belmont,
Missouri, in November 1861, and the following February he captured Forts
Henry and Donelson, along with some thirteen thousand prisoners. Caught
off guard at his encampment at Pittsburg Landing, Grant nonetheless de-
cisively won the Battle of Shiloh (or Pittsburg Landing) the second day.
Although the new general-in-chief was unimpressed with Grant's victory at
Shiloh, after the capture of Corinth, Grant appeared to be waging war and
maintaining Union control within his district. He yearned for wider authority in order to advance toward Vicksburg. Although Halleck was jealous of
his subordinate's successes, he realized that he could continue to take credit
for them.[19]

Option 2

John A. McClernand was born in 1812, and by dint of self-education he was
admitted to the Illinois bar in 1832. He became an Illinois assemblyman and
then served several terms as a member of the United States Congress. In 1860
McClernand was defeated in his effort to become the Speaker of the House
of Representatives. Although his only previous military service had been as a
private in the Black Hawk War in 1832, his political power and influence were
such that Pres. Abraham Lincoln appointed him brigadier general to help
keep southern Illinois Democrats in the Union. McClernand was further

Maj. Gen. John McClernand,
USA. *The Photographic History of
the Civil War*, Vol. X, p. 177.

appointed major general in March 1862, junior to Grant. A political animal, he continuously sought advanced rank and command and blatantly advocated for his cause. By often praising his men's accomplishments, he made sure they reflected positively on him. With some exceptions, the term *political general* became synonymous with *incompetent*. McClernand generally fit right into that category.[20]

Decision

On October 25, per an agreement between Halleck and Secretary of War Edwin M. Stanton, the men appointed U. S. Grant to command the Department of the Tennessee, which included his former district.[21]

Results/Impact

This decision clarified several problems Sam Grant faced. As the new commander of the department, he now controlled actions and events within it. Equally important, he now was able to maintain at least some control and oversight over his budding rival McClernand. The Illinois politician turned general gained permission to raise regiments, some for Grant, but others for a "special force" he would command to move against Vicksburg. This was going to result in conflict between the two generals, but Grant would have the upper hand. Although McClernand would make no critical decisions himself,

Secretary of War Edwin M. Stanton, USA. *The Photographic History of the Civil War*, Vol. X, p. 12.

and he at times was an asset to his senior commander, he managed to remain a real thorn in Grant's side for most of the upcoming campaign.[22]

More importantly, as commander of territory including northern Mississippi, Grant could now focus on what he had been eyeing for months: capturing Vicksburg. The critical decision to appoint Grant commander of the Department of the Tennessee started his efforts to launch the Vicksburg Campaign as we now know it. It is doubtful whether McClernand, Sherman, or any other general would have led the offensive as well as U. S. Grant eventually did, overcoming so many obstacles, as we will see. Without his appointment, the campaign certainly would have gone in another direction.[23]

Davis Fails to Unify Command of the Mississippi River

Situation

From a geographic perspective, a river is logically an obvious, well-defined boundary for a military district or department. There can be little dispute as to where the area of command ends. However, when it comes to defending a river, both sides must be guarded. If an officer secures only one side of a river to control and protect the waterway, he must rely on the cooperation of the commander of the other side of that river. Unfortunately, depending on different leaders of departments on either side of a river is not likely to be as successful as having both sides under the control of one commanding offficer.[24]

Pres. Jefferson Davis designated a series of departments within the Confederacy at the beginning of the Civil War. Some of these were arbitrary and based on geographical or political boundaries, rather than military ones. This was particularly obvious along the Mississippi River. As noted above, Davis assigned Pemberton command of the Department of Mississippi and East Louisiana, which gave him authority over the east bank of the Mississippi. However, the west bank of that river, per Davis's command system, fell under the control of the Trans-Mississippi Department, with Lieut. Gen. Theophilus H. Holmes commanding. In the spring of 1863 Davis replaced Holmes with Lieut. Gen. Edmund Kirby Smith. Cooperation between Confederate departments was typically uncommon, with each commander believing his assignment required all of his troops. Thus, it usually took orders from Richmond to force the transfer of troops from one department to another.[25]

Options

President Davis debated four options concerning control over the Mississippi River. He could leave the command structure as it existed, with each bank under the authority of a different general. He could also consolidate the two banks of the river under one department. Davis could request that Holmes, now commander of the District of Arkansas, reinforce Pemberton. Finally, he could order Holmes to reinforce Pemberton.[26]

Option 1

Of course, the simplest solution was for Davis to maintain the status quo, hoping that each commander would adequately defend his respective side of the river. However, this option would not be satisfactory if the Yankees eventually arrived on the east bank in an attempt to capture Vicksburg. Additional troops would be required to protect the Hill City.[27]

Option 2

Perhaps the best option would be to place both banks of the Mississippi River, along with some additional land on each side, in one department under the command of one general. This officer then could send troops to either or both sides of the river as necessary without requesting help, unless he ultimately needed additional troops from outside his department. Placing one general in command of the area around Vicksburg actually was the logical choice to best defend the city.[28]

Option 3

If Davis kept the departments intact, he could nonetheless request that Holmes reinforce Pemberton with sufficient troops to repulse Grant's advancing Army of the Tennessee. This would otherwise keep the department structures intact for the long haul, while satisfying the temporary necessity of providing enough additional soldiers to confront Grant. The downside, of course, was that this cooperation would be dependent on Holmes's whims as to whether he would loan out part or all of his command. As mentioned above, cooperation between departments and districts was chancy at best.[29]

Option 4

Next to reorganizing the departments, the best way Davis might help was to order Holmes to reinforce Pemberton with a specific number of units from his department. This would ensure that Pemberton had a better opportunity to confront and defeat Grant's army, thereby saving Vicksburg and retaining control of the Mississippi River.[30]

Decision

Unfortunately, politics interfered with Davis's decision. He had preferred to order Holmes to send part of his command to serve under Pemberton. However, the Confederate secretary of war, George W. Randolph, had ordered Holmes to precisely do that without clearing it through the president. Furious, Davis rebuked Randolph, causing his immediate resignation. Having had his pride severely hurt, the president now was unable to give the same order that the secretary had transmitted. Therefore, he let the situation stand by default, leaving the two departments in place and hoping for cooperation between the two department commanders. This failure to act was a blot on the Confederate president's record.[31]

Results/Impact

Sadly for the Confederacy, Holmes refused to cooperate by sending any reinforcements from his district to Pemberton. What he failed to grasp was that if Vicksburg fell to the Union, Arkansas would be of little value to the Confederacy, seriously reducing the effectiveness or necessity of his own command. This is where President Davis actually had the better overall view as to what was more crucial to the survival of his country. Holmes might have been more proactive in defending his side of the river as Grant's corps advanced down the west bank. Because of this decision not to order additional troops from west of the Mississippi, Pemberton was unable to stop Grant's army from invading and eventually capturing his long-sought objective of the bastion of Vicksburg.[32]

Alternate Scenario

One can only wonder how differently the campaign might have evolved had Pemberton assumed command of a new department containing additional troops on the west side of the Mississippi. Reinforced, he might have slowed down or even halted Grant's progress. It would have been even more interesting had Davis directly ordered reinforcements to Pemberton. For instance, might the bloody Battle of Champion Hill have been even bloodier?[33]

CHAPTER 2

GRANT ADVANCES SOUTH THROUGH CENTRAL MISSISSIPPI OCTOBER 26–DECEMBER 30, 1862

Once Maj. Gen. Ulysses S. Grant assumed command of the Department of Tennessee, he made a critical decision as to which approach would be superior for gaining access to Vicksburg and capturing it. Countering his approach, the Confederate high command made a critical decision countervailing the Union movement, significantly altering the direction of the campaign.

Grant Decides to Advance South into Mississippi

Situation

New department commander Maj. Gen. Ulysses S. Grant wasted no time in preparing to advance on the critical bastion of Vicksburg, which dominated the Mississippi River. The Confederates' grip on the city denied the Union a vital supply corridor to the Gulf of Mexico, while also allowing passage of much-needed supplies from the Trans-Mississippi West. This vital location might be accessed from virtually any direction, but each approach posed problems. The department commander had to consider the more viable options.[1]

Options

The most obvious options to assault and capture Vicksburg were traveling down the Mississippi River and directly attacking the city by advancing up the formidable bluffs, or maneuvering to the northeast of the city and then attacking southwest into it. Similar to the second option above, a third course of action was to advance south through the heart of Mississippi and then attack southwest.[2]

Option 1

What seemed to be the simplest means to capture Vicksburg involved taking advantage of the Mississippi River as a conduit to move men, supplies, and ammunition downriver to confront the Confederate bastion. While the river made transportation to the immediate area relatively easy, once the Federals were there, assaulting the formidable city would be difficult. Bluffs several hundred feet above the river provided natural protection and were easily defended. Any attacking force would undoubtedly sustain substantial casualties—perhaps too many for the strike to be successful or even worth the attempt. These were the severe drawbacks to this option.[3]

Option 2

In order to avoid a direct assault on Vicksburg via the bluffs, Federals could maneuver through Chickasaw Bayou northeast of the city, then travel over the Chickasaw Bluffs, allowing troops to approach southwest over high ground. Theoretically, this plan would portend fewer casualties, and once soldiers were onto the high ground, they could assault the bastion. Similar to Option 1, this plan would allow dependable riverboats to provide necessary supplies and transportation. The downside of this option was that it would require establishing a fortified position within the bayou from which the advance on foot could begin.[4]

Option 3

Federal troops could also advance by land south along the Mississippi Central Railroad from the Union supply depot established at Holly Springs, then continue southwest and assault Vicksburg as depicted in Option 2. The disadvantage of this option was its dependence on a long supply line that was only getting longer, and that would be vulnerable to severance by the Confederates.[5]

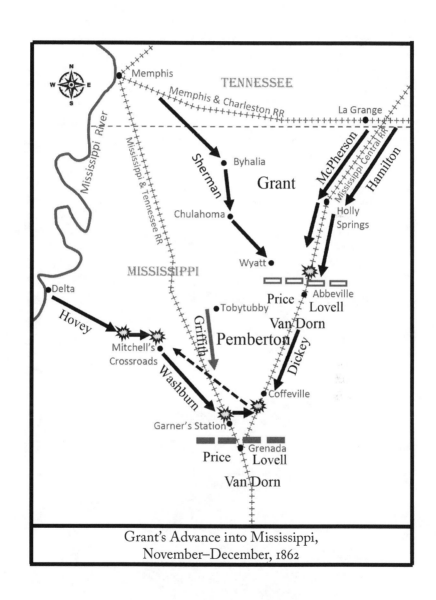

Grant's Advance into Mississippi,
November–December, 1862

Decision

Interestingly, Grant initially decided on Option 3 and followed by adding Option 2. Questioning the general-in-chief Halleck, Sam Grant wanted approval to finally move toward Vicksburg. On November 11, 1862, Halleck replied, "You have command of all troops sent to your department, and have permission to fight the enemy where you please." Grant carefully organized his army and prepared to advance south. The department commander implemented his plan to invade the heart of Mississippi on November 14, 1862. Three divisions had marched out of Corinth and two out of Bolivar, Tennessee, later augmented by three more divisions commanded by Maj. Gen. William T. Sherman. These initial divisions occupied Holly Springs on November 13.[6]

Results/Impact

Advancing along the Mississippi Central Railroad, the invasion force pushed back Confederate troops. By December 2 the Union commander established his headquarters at Oxford. In order to confuse his opponent Pemberton, Grant brought Option 2 into play on the eighth, when he ordered his personal friend Cump Sherman to return to Memphis, then proceed down the Mississippi River to the Yazoo River, move up that river to the Chickasaw Bayou, and advance on the Hill City via the Chickasaw Bluffs to the northeast. Sherman's command was also to move out ahead of Maj. John A. McClernand's potentially competing command. Meanwhile, Pemberton's army continued to retreat to Grenada.[7]

Maj. Gen. William T. Sherman, USA. *The Photographic History of the Civil War*, Vol. X, p. 79.

Grant's plan at this time was to maintain his position at and around Grenada and keep John Pemberton's army dug in along the Yalobusha River. Then Sherman's command could maneuver behind Pemberton's Command and assault the Gibraltar of the West. Unfortunately for the Union, things did not work out as expected. As discussion of the following critical decision will show, the Confederates were eventually able to sever the Federal supply line, forcing Grant's men to retreat. This freed up the Confederate commander to move south and help defend the Hill City from Sherman's assault.[8]

On Christmas Day, after sailing down the Mississippi, Sherman met with Rear Adm. David D. Porter to coordinate the movement up the Yazoo River. They decided to land Cump's army about twelve miles up that river amid some old bayous, including Chickasaw Bayou—as it turned out, not very good ground. This expedition proceeded upriver on the twenty-sixth and landed the next day.[9]

Meanwhile, the Confederates, commanded by Brig. Gen. Stephen D. Lee, quickly shored up their defenses. Observing five locations Sherman would likely assault, Lee fortified them. With good access via a road along the bluffs, the rebel commander could distribute his troops as necessary in order to repel any attacks.[10]

After Sherman's men debarked, they soon grew confused by the terrain and became easy targets for the Confederate defenders. They made virtually no progress on December 28, being repulsed at several locations. Unaware of his department commander's plight, Sherman ordered an all-out offensive for the twenty-ninth. He assaulted the Confederate defenses with his four divisions, but with few locations above water, the various attacking forces were easily picked off by Confederate defenders positioned on and around the Chickasaw Bluffs. It was a disaster. As Sherman himself commented, "I reached Vicksburg at the time appointed, landed, assaulted, and failed." Suffering some 1,776 casualties, he retired. This attempt to capture the Hill City had failed, forcing Grant to devise another plan for its capture.[11]

Confederates Strike Grant's Supply Line

Situation

Department commander Ulysses S. Grant had advanced his army south generally along the Mississippi Central Railroad, forcing John Pemberton's Confederate army farther south. The rebels faced an immensely grave situation. How could they halt the Union commander's approach? The Federal army consisted of five divisions manned by forty thousand soldiers. Confronting this

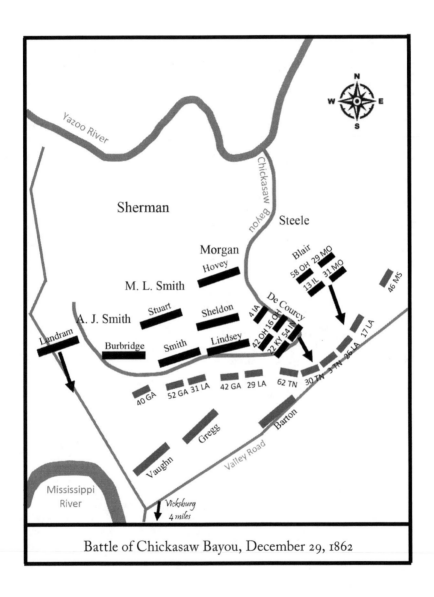

Battle of Chickasaw Bayou, December 29, 1862

show of force were some twenty-four thousand Confederate soldiers, clearly an inadequate number to hold back the advancing blue horde. Complicating the situation, general-in-chief Henry W. Halleck had ordered Brig. Gen. Alvin P. Hovey to conduct a raid into this area of Mississippi. On November 27 Hovey's command of some seven thousand men crossed the Mississippi. On the thirtieth they reached the Mississippi Central Railroad and damaged it as well as telegraph lines. This action forced the Confederates back to the Yalobusha River some fifty miles south of Oxford. Clearly the Union advance had to be stopped, or it would eventually arrive to the northeast of Vicksburg. As noted above, the Confederates were unaware that the Union force presently had no plans to advance farther south.[12]

Options

At this time Pemberton was faced with three options. First, he could beef up his command and, remaining on the defense, slow down and stop the advance of the Federal army. Second, he could retreat farther south while looking for a suitable defensive position, and perhaps round up some additional troops. Finally, he could attempt to sever the Union supply line.[13]

Option 1

If there were any Confederate troops available to join Pemberton's command, this would give that Confederate general better odds of stopping the Federal advance. However, where exactly were these additional soldiers? It seemed unlikely that more men were immediately obtainable.[14]

Option 2

Continuing to slowly retreat would stretch Grant's supply line even farther, assuming he kept advancing south. At some point the Union might not be able to receive enough supplies and ammunition to proceed. Also, additional delays to this advance might allow Pemberton to find other forces to augment his smaller command.[15]

Option 3

If the Confederate command could find a way to sever the Federal supply line, this would most likely force Grant to retreat into Union-held territory and abandon his advance. Sixth Texas Cavalry commander Lieut. Col. John Griffith and some other officers of the First Texas Cavalry Brigade proposed conducting a cavalry raid into the Union rear. Further, they suggested that

Maj. Gen. Earl Van Dorn lead a cavalry command consisting of three to four thousand men.[16]

Decision

John Pemberton quickly agreed with his cavalry commanders to authorize a raid into the Union rear. As suggested, he placed Earl Van Dorn in command of the designated horsemen. Van Dorn selected the cavalry brigades of Lieut. Col. John S. Griffith (who had concocted the plan for the raid), Col. William H. "Red" Jackson, and Col. Robert McCulloch to participate. Numbering 1,500, 1,200, and 800 men respectively, Van Dorn's newly appointed command totaled about 3,500 well-armed troopers. Early on the morning of December 16 the designated force departed Grenada on what would be their leader's finest hour.[17]

Results/Impact

Earl Van Dorn kept his target, Grant's large supply depot at Holly Springs, as secret as possible. He first maneuvered his cavalry force to the east toward Houston, Mississippi, not only to avoid confronting the Union far left, but also to confuse the enemy as to his destination. Successfully evading the Federals, the troopers turned north. Van Dorn briefly contended with a small Yankee cavalry force but rode away from it, surprising his men, who were

Maj. Gen. Earl Van Dorn,
CSA. *The Photographic History of the Civil War*, Vol. X, p. 251.

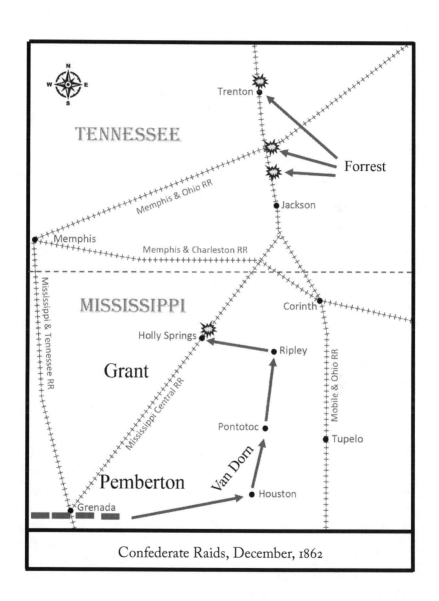

Confederate Raids, December, 1862

still uninformed of their target. Sam Grant had been focused on Brig. Gen. Nathan B. Forrest's cavalry command, which was approaching Jackson, Tennessee, and closing in on the critical Union supply line. When he learned of the enemy cavalry operating near Pontotoc, the Union commander quickly sent out a force to pursue these Confederates. Grant also informed his commanders at Holly Springs, and at Davis's Mill, Grand Junction, La Grange, and Bolivar, Tennessee, to be prepared to defend the Union supply line.[18]

Late on December 19, Van Dorn rode through Pine Grove, only twenty miles east of his destination, Holly Springs. After giving the illusion that they were en route to Bolivar, Van Dorn's men returned to Pine Grove and then advanced west in the darkness toward Holly Springs. Taking every precaution to remain undetected, the Confederate cavalry continued to ride west. Federal supply depot commander Col. Robert C. Murphy, was unaware of their approach, and he decided he would worry about any enemy in the morning. Outside Holly Springs the Confederate commander split his force in two and advanced to the town.[19]

At the break of dawn on the twentieth, the Confederate cavalry rode into Holly Springs virtually unopposed after capturing the Union sentinels. Van Dorn sent Jackson's and McCulloch's Brigades into the town on Salem Street and then to the fairgrounds, where the Second Illinois Cavalry was encamped, quickly overrunning the Federals. A part of those Confederates moved south, invading the camp of the 101st Illinois Infantry, which was defending the railroad depot. Griffith's Texas brigade assisted in the rout at the depot and then rode into downtown, capturing the entire location, as well as Colonel Murphy. Van Dorn's command then proceeded to destroy over $1 million worth of supplies accumulated there in support of Grant's advance south along the Mississippi Central Railroad. It was a huge victory for the Confederacy and a disaster for the Union.[20]

Because Pemberton authorized the successful raid, Grant was forced to withdraw back to northern Mississippi and Tennessee. The Union commander's first attempt to capture the garrison at Vicksburg failed; the Confederates compromised his line of supply, and he could no longer sustain his command deep in Mississippi. Van Dorn's raid had two specific results for Sam Grant. First, he would have to find another avenue of approach to the Hill City in order to capture it. Second, he discovered a new tactic. As his men retreated northward, they began to forage on their own because the Union supply line was no longer capable of supplying the army. The Federals quickly discovered that abundant supplies were available as they retraced their way north. Not only could they generally keep themselves adequately provided with food, but they could also take the war to the very civilians supporting it. This ability to depend on foraging gave Grant a new methodology for future movements on his objective of Vicksburg.[21]

As for the commanding officer of the Holly Springs supply depot, Col. Robert C. Murphy, Ulysses Grant had forgiven him at Iuka for losing provisions there. However, after the debacle at Holly Springs, the colonel would not receive another chance to prove his competence. On January 8, 1863, Grant cashiered him, effective the day of the raid, December 20, because of his "cowardly and disgraceful conduct."[22]

CHAPTER 3

GRANT ADVANCES DOWN THE WEST SIDE OF THE MISSISSIPPI JANUARY–APRIL 1863

After the major setback created by the Holly Spring raid, Maj. Gen. Ulysses S. Grant had to rethink his plan to capture Vicksburg and open up the Mississippi River to Union traffic. He tried four different plans to do so, but they all ultimately failed. He would finally make the critical decision to bypass the Hill City downriver on the west bank, with the help of Rear Adm. David D. Porter.

Grant Advances down the West Side of the Mississippi

Situation

After the raid on Holly Springs and Maj. Gen. William T. Sherman's defeat at the Battle of Chickasaw Bayou, Sam Grant realized that he must use another approach to seize Vicksburg. Over the course of four months, from January to April 1863, he made four new attempts to advance to the Hill City. Unfortunately, all of these failed.[1]

Grant's first attempt was to rework a canal started in the summer of 1862 by Brig. Gen. Thomas Williams per orders from Maj. Gen. Benjamin F. Butler, military governor of New Orleans. As the river made a 180-degree turn at Vicksburg, a short neck existed across Young's Point. The theory was that if the canal was dug and completed, upon opening the upriver entrance, the Mississippi River would alter its flow into the new canal. Grant believed there was no harm in completing the work abandoned by Williams, a task that would also keep his men occupied during what would otherwise be downtime. With some four thousand soldiers at work, the Federals relocated the upriver entrance to the canal and proceeded to enlarge it. In late February, the river broke through the northern entrance and flooded the unfinished project. By March most everyone, including Sam Grant, realized the modified passageway simply was not a viable option. Interestingly, several years later, the river rechanneled itself through the canal on its own![2]

Doubting the viability of the canal project, Grant looked elsewhere to bypass Vicksburg. On January 30 he ordered a levee cut on the Mississippi River leading into Lake Providence. Beginning on February 4, he spent several days with Maj. Gen. James B. McPherson, an experienced engineering officer, to explore a potential water route that existed some four hundred miles south, eventually flowing into the Red River and then back into the Mississippi just above Port Hudson. The Union commander quickly realized this was an unlikely avenue of approach, but he again thought it would keep his men occupied. Grant eventually abandoned the scheme.[3]

Union troops made yet another attempt on Vicksburg, only this time from the north. A few miles south of Helena, Arkansas, on the east side of the Mississippi was Yazoo Pass. Moon Lake and the Coldwater River were connected to it. The Coldwater River flowed south into the Tallahatchie River, which joined the Yalobusha River at Greenwood, which became the Yazoo River. In order to protect plantations along the Mississippi River from flooding, the State of Mississippi had placed a strong levee across the entrance to Yazoo Pass. Removing that levee might allow Union gunboats access to territory near Grenada, and all the way to the area around Chickasaw Bayou. Grant sent his staff member and engineer Lieut. Col. James Wilson to Helena to verify that this was the case. On February 3 a hole was made in the levee there, and water rushed in.[4]

On February 24 a Union division commanded by Brig. Gen. Leonard Ross moved via transports into the waterway. On March 11 the expedition arrived at Greenwood only to discover a major problem. The Confederates had erected a fort (Pemberton) with its left flank on the Yazoo and its right flank on the Tallahatchie, thus blocking further movement downriver. The Federals

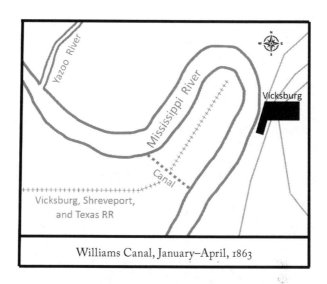

Williams Canal, January–April, 1863

Lake Providence Route, February–March, 1863

Yazoo Pass Expedition, February–April, 1863

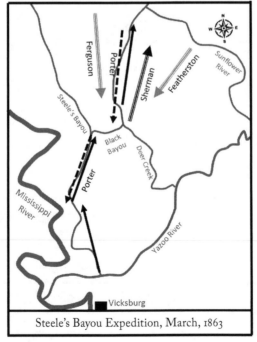

Steele's Bayou Expedition, March, 1863

tried several times to assault and bombard Fort Pemberton, including by cutting an additional levee. But after March 16 the invasion force retreated, as it was unable to reduce the fort.[5]

Grant authorized a final attempt to approach Vicksburg via the high ground to its northeast; this plan was originally suggested by Admiral Porter. A much shorter route below Fort Pemberton apparently existed. The admiral's plan was to steam from the Mississippi River into the Yazoo and then turn north into Steele's Bayou. This would avoid Confederate artillery on the bluffs to the south. The Federals would then continue north past Cypress Lake into Black Bayou. At the junction with Deer Creek, their journey would continue farther north to the junction with the Rolling Fork River. Turning south, the proposed route next flowed into the Sunflower River, which continued to Yazoo City. This portion of the approach involved a couple of hundred miles of steaming to end up twenty miles from the Hill City. From this point, Union forces could either advance north to Fort Pemberton and capture it from the rear, or they could move directly toward Vicksburg from the higher ground northeast of that city.[6]

Unfortunately, the theory of the plan was more optimistic than the reality. On March 16 Grant accompanied Porter about thirty miles into the interior, then authorized the movement. The admiral ultimately departed with five gunboats, a force augmented with part of Sherman's command. The Federals encountered obstructions, narrow passageways, and eventually Confederate resistance. Overhanging trees felled the ships' smokestacks, and snakes made their way onboard. Finally stuck, with the Confederates blocking retreat, Porter called for help from Cump's men. After marching all night, they saved the naval force, allowing it to back down the river on March 22. While these attempts to reach Vicksburg all failed, author J. E. C. Fuller comments, "He [Grant] waged three months of toilsome warfare in the swamps of the Mississippi because these conditions demanded activity, and simultaneously he converted this waste of tactical energy into a strategic smoke cloud to cover his eventual advance." This final failure led to the Union commander's next critical decision.[7]

Options

At this time Grant determined that he had three choices. The first was to position his combined land and naval force in the best location to directly assault Vicksburg. Second, he could move back to Memphis and, from there, retrace the movement he had made last fall, advancing south along the Mississippi Central Railroad. Finally, he could travel down the west side of the Mississippi, bypassing Vicksburg, and then cross over the river south of his target.[8]

Option 1

Although the simplest choice in theory, a direct assault on the formidable bastion of Vicksburg would at best be a very bloody one with a huge number of casualties. Again, Grant undoubtedly spent little time considering this option.[9]

Option 2

Another logical way to advance on Vicksburg entailed moving back to Memphis and then advancing south along the Mississippi Central Railroad. This time Grant's supply line would have to be strongly protected. Its defense would require a significant number of troops, reducing the commander's ability to assault the city upon arrival there. The political downside to this option was that moving north to Memphis would make it appear to the Northern public that Grant was retreating. He could not accept this vision and reasonably expect to keep his command.[10]

Option 3

While awaiting the results of the four separate attempts to move on Vicksburg, Grant had begun to realize that he must consider a different movement to eventually capture the city. The only new option was to advance down the west side of the Mississippi River, avoiding a confrontation with the defenders of the Hill City. However, once past the city Grant would need to cross over to the east bank. That would be a problem.[11]

Decision

Although the exact date when U. S. Grant made the decision is unknown, by April he had chosen Option 3 and ordered preparations to advance down the west side of the Mississippi River.[12]

Results/Impact

By April 2 Grant was organizing his movement down the river. This critical decision resulted in the plan of attack on Vicksburg that would finally come to fruition, leading to perhaps the finest successful military campaign ever conducted in the continental United States. However, there was one very critical problem that must be overcome: How would the Union troops recross to the east bank of the Mississippi? This question engendered the following critical decision.[13]

Porter Agrees to Run Past Vicksburg

Situation

Ulysses Grant and David Porter had established a good working relationship—not necessarily a likely possibility due to jealousies between the army and navy. As noted above, Porter had cooperated with the Union commander on several occasions, unfortunately without much success so far. When Grant finally decided to advance down the west side of the Mississippi River, he knew he had to overcome one enormous logistical problem. Once his troops had successfully bypassed Vicksburg along the west bank of the Mississippi River, he needed to move them back across the river in order to advance on the city. The only logical way Grant could conduct this crossing was by riverboat—in fact, by many riverboats. These, of course, were commanded by Admiral Porter. This placed the naval officer in a bit of a quandary.[14]

Options

Porter had two options: he could either attempt to run the batteries located at Vicksburg, whose purpose was to halt any attempt at a Union movement past them, or he could decline to take that chance.[15]

Rear Adm. David D. Porter, USA.
The Photographic History of the Civil War,
Vol. VI, p. 195.

Option 1

Prior to this time a few Union navy craft had successfully run past the Vicksburg batteries. However, additional batteries were now in place, and any Union vessel making the attempt stood the chance of being severely damaged or sunk. It certainly did not appear feasible for unarmed transports to try and sneak past the Confederate bastion.[16]

Additionally, Porter realized that, assuming his flotilla could somehow survive passing the batteries, these craft could not return north past the same batteries. The somewhat swift river current would assist passage south because of its north-to-south flow, increasing the ships' actual speed and lessening the time they spent actually passing the batteries. However, sailing north the vessels would fight the current, with their actual speed reduced to just a few knots. The slower pace would make them targets for the Confederate batteries for a much longer period, severely reducing the likelihood of successful travel upstream. Thus these craft would be left in sort of a no-man's-land south of Vicksburg, and north of Confederate-controlled Port Hudson farther south.[17]

Option 2

Given the daunting possibility that Confederates could sink or severely damage whatever gunboats and transports that attempted to run past the Vicksburg batteries, the safest decision would be simply not to undertake the movement Grant requested. Another major consideration for Rear Admiral Porter would be the potential loss of those killed or wounded during the attempted passage.[18]

Decision

With plenty of reasons not to comply with Grant's request, Porter nonetheless agreed to try to run past the Confederate batteries at Vicksburg.[19]

Results/Impact

Grant considered Porter's naval command indispensable for his movement down the west side of the Mississippi River to succeed. The admiral's acquiescence allowed the Union commander to move forward with his plans. As noted above, gunboats, transports, and supply barges would be necessary to supply the Federal force below Vicksburg and provide transportation back across the river to its east bank. While Union gunboats had passed the Confederate batteries before, this was a major challenge and very risky in nature.[20]

The Union naval commander went to work preparing his various craft to best survive the run past the Confederate batteries trained on the river. He ordered the gunboats to be protected with bales of cotton and hay. Additionally, the steam exhaust was diverted into the paddle-wheel housing in order to diminish the engine noise. Additional safeguards included attaching barges of coal to the left (port) side (nearest the batteries) of the gunboats to absorb artillery fire, and placing necessary equipment in barges attached to the less vulnerable right (starboard) side of the vessels. All lighting was extinguished to provide maximum concealment.[21]

Bad weather forced postponement of the try until the night of April 16. Initially the Union craft proceeded undetected. The admiral led six armed gunboats (his flagship *Benton*, followed by the *Lafayette, Louisville, Mound City, Pittsburg,* and *Carondelet*), three army transports (the *Silver Wave, Henry Clay,* and *Forest Queen*), and a seventh gunboat (the *Tuscumbia*). Onboard the gunboats were a combined seventy-nine cannon. An ammunition barge was cut adrift to float on its own behind the fleet. However, once discovered, the Confederates lit fires on the west side of the river to silhouette the Yankees. The batteries opened up in the attempt to halt the Federals' passing. Some thirty-seven large-caliber cannon, seventeen rifled and twenty smoothbore, went into action, aided by another thirteen smaller fieldpieces. Because most of the Confederate cannon were unable to fire low, Porter ordered his command to sail close to the eastern Mississippi shore, giving his command better odds. He also ordered the gunboats to return fire, which destroyed many buildings along the Vicksburg waterfront. The combined Confederate firepower eventually hit a coal barge, forcing the sailors to cut it loose. Soon, other coal barges were also cut loose to improve maneuvering.[22]

Porter's fleet successfully made it past the Hill City batteries. Only one unarmed transport, the *Henry Clay*, was actually lost; although some of them were heavily damaged, all the others were soon available for Grant's use below the city. Interestingly, Assistant Secretary of War Charles Dana counted 525 cannon shots![23]

Overall, the Union commander was so pleased with the success of this run past the Vicksburg batteries that he ordered another attempt. After more extensive preparation, six transports (the *Tigress, Anglo-Saxon, J. W. Cheeseman, Moderator, Horizon,* and *Empire City*) and twelve barges moved downriver past the alert batteries on the night of April 22. Manned by soldier volunteers, this fleet also successfully made the trip, losing only the *Tigress* (Grant's command boat at Shiloh) to enemy fire. With the help and support of Porter, Sam Grant was now ready to cross the river and assault Vicksburg. The US Navy's cooperation allowed the campaign to continue as planned.[24]

Alternate Scenario

Had Admiral Porter kept his gunboats and other craft free from danger by not cooperating with Grant, the Union commander could not have eventually crossed the river. Of necessity, Grant would have forced himself to find another method of approach to Vicksburg, one requiring an entirely different form of campaign. It is still likely that Grant would have eventually captured the Hill City, but a different campaign certainly would have altered Civil War history.[25]

CHAPTER 4

GRANT PREPARES TO ADVANCE ON VICKSBURG
APRIL 30–MAY 3, 1863

Two critical decisions, both made by Maj. Gen. Ulysses S. Grant, altered his initial plans after Rear Adm. David D. Porter successfully ran transport vessels and gunboats past the Vicksburg batteries. A third critical decision, partially due to Grant's suggestion, involved diversionary efforts by the Union to confuse Confederate commander Lieut. Gen. John C. Pemberton. These decisions contributed to the ultimate success of Grant's Vicksburg Campaign.

Grant Decides to Land at Bruinsburg

Situation

Before we discuss this critical decision, we need to briefly examine the role of Maj. Gen. John McClernand in this campaign. McClernand made no critical decisions (as we will see, this was fortunate for Sam Grant). Nevertheless, he was often insubordinate to Grant, and he made a determined attempt to gain command of his own Union army to advance to and capture Vicksburg.[1]

As briefly described earlier, McClernand was born on May 30, 1812, in Kentucky, but his family moved to Illinois soon after. Interestingly, his career often followed that of Abraham Lincoln. The mostly self-educated

McClernand was admitted to the Illinois bar in 1832. He later served as a private in the Black Hawk War and represented Illinois for several terms in the United States Congress. He was bombastic and anti-abolitionist, and he favored Jacksonian principles. McClernand was defeated in a run for Speaker of the House of Representatives in 1860 because of his moderate sentiments on slavery and secession. Yet he retained the goodwill of his constituents, making him a formidable power within critical southern Illinois, or "Little Egypt," a region prone to identify with the Confederacy. Thus President Lincoln needed McClernand's political pull to keep that part of Illinois supporting the Union. Therefore, on May 17, 1861, Lincoln appointed him, a man with no military command experience, brigadier general of volunteers.[2]

Lincoln had appointed U. S. Grant brigadier general retroactive to May 17, but he was ranked nineteenth, while McClernand was ranked thirty-third on the same list. At the small Battle of Belmont, fought on November 7, 1861, Grant's ranking gave him overall command, with John McClernand leading a brigade under him. At the Battle of Fort Donelson McClernand then commanded a division, also under Grant. During the following Battle of Shiloh, McClernand again fought well but apparently became convinced he could do better. He then began to lobby for an independent command while placed on recruiting duty in lower Illinois.[3]

The Illinois politician finally received his wish on October 21, 1862, when he was ordered to recruit troops and send them south, where he was authorized to advance on Vicksburg. Yet McClernand still remained under the authority of the department commander, U. S. Grant. As head of the department, Grant sent the troops recruited by McClernand to Maj. Gen. William T. Sherman, who used them with his own in the failed assault at Chickasaw Bayou in late December 1862. Although incensed by this "trickery," McClernand did eventually lead a successful advance on Helena, Arkansas, with Sherman under his command. Grant had quickly recognized that he must be physically in the area and in overall command in order to protect his friend Sherman and control the political general McClernand.[4]

To the disgust of Grant, Sherman, and Porter, McClernand was always congratulating his men (and himself) and finagling for independent command, further glory, and political capitalism. Nonetheless, McClernand apparently satisfied Grant that he could and would fight when ordered. As we will see, the Union commander selected the political general to lead the advance downriver past Vicksburg and then toward Jackson, Mississippi. McClernand's men would form the left flank and most exposed of the three Union corps, with this position surprisingly keeping Sherman in the middle and the inexperienced Maj. Gen. James B. McPherson on the safer right

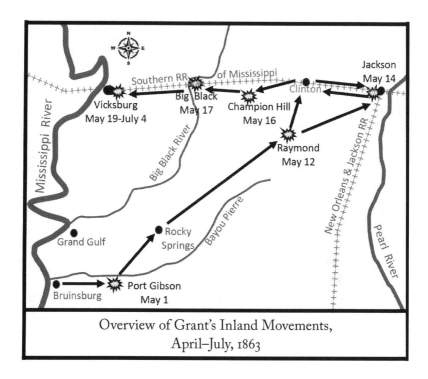

Overview of Grant's Inland Movements,
April–July, 1863

flank. Considering the lack of rapport between these men, that is quite an interesting positioning of his corps. Nevertheless, Grant attempted to keep close watch on McClernand.[5]

Therefore, and probably for the reasons described above, on March 29 U. S. Grant ordered the Illinois politician's four-division corps to begin advancing down the west side of the Mississippi River. The movement commenced on the thirty-first. Grant hoped this was the beginning of his new attempt to approach the Hill City. However, it was not until Porter's successful runs past the Gibraltar of the West's batteries that Grant was comfortable with his latest plan.[6]

While the advance down the west side was fraught with obstacles because of the high waters, Union troops began building bridges along the levees, the only places above water, and corduroying roads. Here everyone marched, camped, watched out for Confederates, and buried the dead, largely from disease. It was miserable duty.[7]

Sam Grant's plan was to gather his command at Hard Times, Louisiana, which was directly west of the Confederate batteries at Grand Gulf, some thirty miles below Vicksburg. Then he would reduce the batteries located there and land his troops. The town was named for a large whirlpool (or gulf) formed by the Mississippi River and flowing against a large rocky bluff. Two well-protected forts were located there with parapets forty feet above the river and forty feet thick. Forts Wade and Cobun were heavily armed and supported with additional fieldpieces. On April 29, seven Union gunboats steamed to and began to bombard the forts at Grand Gulf. Around 7:50 a.m. the vessels commenced firing. For some five and a half hours they poured shot and shell on the strongholds and succeeded in silencing the guns of Fort Wade. However, the gunboats were unable to do the same with Fort Cobun. Roughly 2,500 Federal projectiles were fired on the citadels! Finally accepting defeat around 1:15 p.m., the fleet returned west. The Union commander's plan for crossing over the river and landing at Grand Gulf was no longer practicable. The Federals now required a different location to land on the east side of the river.[8]

Options

A disappointed Grant now realized that he must find and designate a new place to land his command to commence his advance against Vicksburg. He knew that it was imperative for the landing site to provide adequate docking for the transports bringing the troops over. In addition, the site needed good access to roads that led east into the interior and, perhaps most importantly, remained undefended by Confederates. Two locations quickly came under consideration: Rodney and Bruinsburg.[9]

Option 1

Rodney, located below Vicksburg, appeared to meet the criteria for a place to unload Grant's command. Here, a road led east toward Port Gibson, presenting the general with a good possibility of success.[10]

Option 2

However, Grant discovered another viable location. A "colored man" came to the Union commander that evening and indicated that Bruinsburg was a good landing place. This spot was located some ten miles north of Rodney, and it featured a good road leading about twelve miles to Port Gibson, meaning the Federals would travel less distance than they would from Rodney.[11]

Decision

The key to either option was the likelihood, or lack thereof, of Confederate resistance to the landing of the Federal force. The effect of enemy opposition on amphibious landings was graphically displayed on D-day, June 6, 1944, during the initial phase of Operation Overlord. The Axis forces confronted Allied forces landing in Normandy, quickly inflicting a great number of fatalities on the invading troops. The Allies sustained almost five thousand casualties from sea and air that day. Although this event certainly was not historically relevant to Sam Grant, being far in the future, the general nonetheless wished to avoid a similar situation. He designated Bruinsburg as the landing site for his command.[12]

Results/Impact

John McClernand's Thirteenth Corps, consisting of four divisions, prepared to cross over the Mississippi. Loaded onto the transports, some seventeen thousand troops in all rode these craft to Bruinsburg on the eastern shore. The men were considerably concerned, for what if the landing was contested? Fortunately, the initial soldiers on the ground found no Confederates and "captured" the only civilian present at the landing. It was imperative that this command move immediately to the bluffs, about a mile inland, in order to safely establish their bridgehead. However, McClernand had forgotten to supply his troops with the necessary three days' worth of rations. A frustrated Grant tried to maintain his composure while the required supplies were brought over. The Thirteenth Corps, less the cavalry, finally advanced inland at 4:00 p.m., followed by a division of James B. McPherson's Seventeenth Corps. One of the largest and most successful amphibious landings in history had been completed! The Vicksburg Campaign continued to be successful, allowing Grant to continue to advance into Mississippi.[13]

A much relieved U. S. Grant wrote of the Bruinsburg landing years later in his *Personal Memoirs*:

> When this was effected I felt a degree of relief scarcely ever
> since equalled [*sic*] since. Vicksburg was not yet taken it
> is true, nor were its defenders demoralized by any of our
> previous moves. I was now in the enemy's country, with a
> vast river and the stronghold of Vicksburg between me and
> my base of supplies. But I was on dry ground on the same
> side of the river with the enemy. All the campaigns, labors,
> hardships, and exposures from the month of December

previous to this time that had been made and endured, were for the accomplishment of this one object.[14]

However, as we will see next, another critical decision had directly contributed to the Union success.

Grierson's Raid and Other Diversions Confuse Pemberton

Situation

As an editorial note, Col. Benjamin Grierson's raid and the other three diversions all began prior to Grant's successful landing at Bruinsburg. However, since their cumulative effect was the lack of Confederate opposition on April 30 to the disembarkment at Bruinsburg, these events are presented chronologically out of order here.

Apparently, Grant strongly believed in the use of diversionary maneuvers to mask his primary movements and surprise his enemy. Once he had made the critical decision to advance down the west side of the Mississippi River, he sought means to hide or confuse the Confederate high command as to his actual intention. Could distracting raids be possible, and could they succeed?[15]

Perhaps the most important of the raids began back on February 12, 1863, at his headquarters in Memphis. Both Maj. Gen. Charles H. Hamilton and Grant suggested to Maj. Gen. Stephen A. Hurlbut, commander of the Sixteenth Corps in the Army of the Tennessee, that the Confederate cavalry's temporary absence from the area made it a great time to conduct a cavalry raid south "to strike the Vicksburg and Jackson [rail]road." Coincidently, Sam Grant told Hurlbut the next day, "It seems to me that [Col. Benjamin] Grierson, with about 500 picked men, might succeed in making his way south and cut the railroad east of Jackson, Miss. The undertaking would be a hazardous one, but it would pay well if carried out. I do not direct that this shall be done, but leave it for a volunteer enterprise."[16]

Options

Hurlbut thus faced a critical decision. He could either authorize the raid proposed by both Hamilton and Grant, or he could defer it based on the high likelihood of failure.[17]

Option 1

The proposed cavalry raid would likely accomplish several positive results if successful. It would confuse the Confederate high command as to the Federals' objective(s). It would also force rebel units, perhaps both cavalry and infantry, to respond by pursuing and capturing the members of the raiding party. With any luck, the Union troopers could destroy at least some part or parts of the Confederate railroad system, so important for the carriage of soldiers, ammunition, and supplies. The downside of this plan was the possibility that the cavalrymen would fail to carry out the proposed destruction, and the chance that part or all of the force would be captured, costing the Federals manpower. [18]

Option 2

Although always an exciting enterprise, a cavalry raid required a great deal of planning and coordination. The proper choice of commanders and troops to ensure success was a must. Examination of potential response by the enemy would strongly influence the possibility of a favorable result. Finally, the weather, condition of the roads, and just plain good or bad luck might ruin an otherwise worthy attempt. These factors would force the Union command to not simply take a chance on a raid. [19]

Decision

After thoroughly evaluating the pros and cons of the possibility of success of a raid, Hurlbut initially postponed it because of Confederate activity. Grant expressed disappointment. However, the Sixteenth Corps commander eventually ordered the raid to commence. Col. Benjamin Grierson was a well-respected cavalry commander and the logical choice to command the raid. [20]

Results/Impact

Grierson's raid began early on April 17, as his command left La Grange, Tennessee, and it successfully concluded sixteen days later on May 2, in Baton Rouge, Louisiana. The raid made its mark on history in several ways. First, at least initially, it thoroughly confused the Confederate high command as to the line of march and objectives of the raid. Second, on April 24 Grierson's men successfully completed part of their mission when they cut the Southern Railroad of Mississippi at Newton Station, east of Jackson. Most importantly, pertaining to Grant's campaign, the raid's movements drew pursuing Confederate cavalry away from the Union landing point at Bruinsburg. As a result, the Union commander successfully landed some twenty-two thousand troops without any immediate Confederate resistance, facilitating Federal movements to establish a beachhead and then advance inland. After fighting near Port Gibson, Sam Grant and his command, being reinforced with the

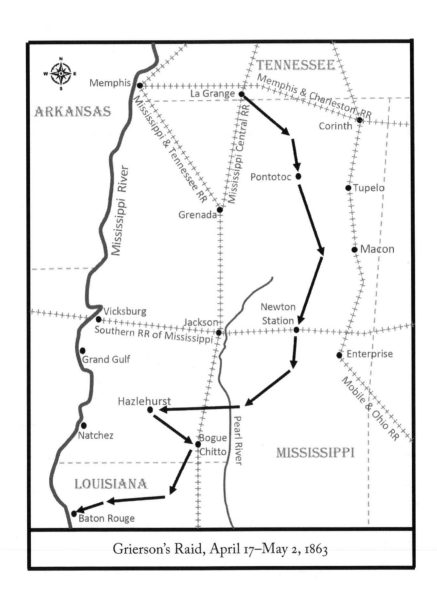

Grierson's Raid, April 17–May 2, 1863

Col. Benjamin Grierson, USA.
The Photographic History of the Civil War, Vol. IV, p. 133.

rest of McPherson's and then Sherman's corps, finally positioned themselves where Grant had been wishing to be for months. The general quickly established a supply depot at Grand Gulf, which had been abandoned by then.[21]

Although Grierson's raid was the most dramatic one, several others confused the Confederate high command even further. Col. Abel Streight sought to take four infantry regiments, including his own Seventy-First Indiana, mount them on mules, and advance east to disrupt the logistically important Western and Atlantic Railroad. This command departed Nashville on April 11 and reached Tuscumbia, Alabama, on the twenty-sixth. Quickly overcome by Brig. Gen. Nathan B. Forrest's pursuing cavalry, Streight surrendered to the Confederate cavalryman at Cedar Bluff, Alabama, on May 3.

Although Streight's raid ultimately failed in its objective, it drew Forrest far away from Mississippi, helping keep the landing at Bruinsburg clear. Additionally, these strikes kept Pemberton and the Confederate commanders confused, allowing Grant to land unopposed and begin his campaign in earnest.[22]

Grant ordered two additional movements designed to perplex Pemberton. He directed Maj. Gen. Frederick Steele to advance to Greenville, Mississippi, and Sherman to feint to Snyder's Bluff. These movements contributed to Pemberton's confusion, again resulting in the Confederates' failure to block Grant's landing at Bruinsburg.[23]

Grant Decides Not to Support Banks

Situation

As described above, Grant successfully landed his initial force at Bruinsburg and advanced inland. He continued to order reinforcements from the rest of McPherson's Seventeenth Corps and eventually Sherman's Fifteenth Corps. Confederate Brig. Gen. John Bowen, a competent commander, quickly positioned his four brigades to contest the Union advance toward Port Gibson. The many gullies and dense vegetation near the small town favored the defense. However, Bowen had only some seven thousand men to stop an approaching Federal force about three times as large. By May 2 the Yankees had captured Port Gibson, and Bowen was forced to retreat. The Union now had a solid foothold on Mississippi soil, and the small Confederate command manning Grand Gulf was quickly turned out of position. As he had previously desired, Grant made this location his supply depot. While his troops continued to arrive, and while he awaited additional supplies, the Union commander continued to consider his alternatives.[24]

Vicksburg tends to receive most of the credit for single-handedly keeping the Union from using the Mississippi River. In reality, however, Port Hudson, about 27 river miles north of Baton Rouge and some 240 river miles south of the Hill City, was a key detriment to Federal passage. As long as these two bastions maintained control of the river, Union commerce remained at a standstill, and the Confederacy could ship valuable supplies such as meat and soldiers from its territory west of the river. While Grant concentrated on the capture of Vicksburg, Maj. Gen. Nathaniel P. Banks determined to wrest Port Hudson from Confederate control. As commander of the Department of New Orleans, Banks had replaced Maj. Gen. Benjamin "Beast" Butler, who had dealt harshly with the secessionist citizens of that city. On December 17, 1862, Banks reoccupied Baton Rouge and planned to recover Port Hudson for the Union. However, he quickly became entangled with the bureaucracy of occupying the largest Confederate city.[25]

General Banks was born in Waltham, Massachusetts, on January 30, 1816. Although he had little formal education, he was admitted to the bar. Subsequently, he became a member of the Massachusetts legislature after many attempts, and he was elected speaker of that house in 1855. Banks parlayed his position as a state legislator into a seat in the United States Congress that same year. The next year, he was elected speaker of the US House of Representatives. In 1858 Banks was elected governor of Massachusetts, serving in that position until January 1861, when President Lincoln appointed him a

Maj. Gen. Nathaniel Banks, USA. *The
Photographic History of the Civil War*,
Vol. X, p. 177.

major general. With apparently no military experience, Banks undoubtedly
rankled many Union officers due to his high rank. However, his political
background and support for the Union required Lincoln to place him in high
command, where he could contribute to the cause by bringing in recruits,
money, and propaganda. Banks demonstrated his military inability when
Maj. Gen. Thomas "Stonewall" Jackson expelled him and his command from
the Shenandoah Valley in late 1861, and again when Jackson defeated him
at Cedar Mountain in August 1862. Postdating the Vicksburg Campaign,
Nathaniel Banks would be most remembered for his bungled Red River
Campaign of 1864.[26]

While commanders on both sides quickly assumed that he would move
to assault Port Hudson, Banks focused his attention elsewhere. Rear Adm.
David G. Farragut decided to try to run past the batteries at Port Hudson,
hopefully assisted by some of Banks's troops. On the night of March 14–15
Farragut attempted to do so, resulting in only two of his gunboats successfully passing north of the batteries. This outcome influenced Banks to turn
his attention to southwestern Louisiana. Due to several factors, including
poor communication between Banks and Grant referencing the potential
capture of Port Hudson did not help the situation.[27]

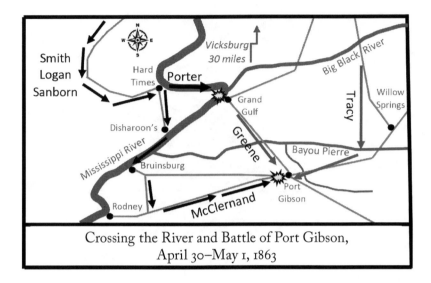

Crossing the River and Battle of Port Gibson,
April 30–May 1, 1863

Options

After successfully winning the small battle for Port Gibson, Grant had time to catch up on his personal hygiene, arrange for a new supply line to get established, and await reinforcements, especially Sherman's corps. Additionally, he faced another decision that involved both general-in-chief Halleck and Nathaniel Banks. The original plan was for the Union commander to send Maj. Gen. John McClernand's Thirteenth Corps to assist Banks in capturing Port Hudson. However, this would deprive Grant of one of his three corps, now deep in enemy territory. So his options were to either send the Illinois politician's corps south to Banks, or to keep it with the rest of his army.[28]

Option 1

Per prior arrangement, Halleck and Banks agreed that Grant would send McClernand's corps south to aid in the capture of Port Hudson. This would most likely require a month's time. As a result, this loan of troops would deprive the Union commander of roughly one-third of his force while located deep in enemy territory. He would either have to either sit around, waiting for McClernand's return, or he would have to maneuver in Confederate country with his sizably reduced army. Sam Grant held the initiative, and it would be shameful for him to lose it then.[29]

Option 2

Rather than lose McClernand, Grant could retain him and his corps and more confidently begin to maneuver to capture Vicksburg. Both Halleck and Grant saw through Banks's diversionary mini-campaigns, which didn't seem pertinent to the Vicksburg–Port Hudson situation. Also, since Banks ranked Grant, would he eventually give McClernand's corps back to Grant, or keep it for further use?[30]

Decision

On May 3 U. S. Grant firmly decided that he would Keep McClernand's corps and use it as best he could in his advance on Vicksburg.[31]

Results/Impact

Reducing the size of his command in the face of the enemy seemed a poor choice for Grant, and he planned his next move using all three of his corps. The result has often been labeled Grant's blitzkrieg. Technically this label is incorrect as a blitzkrieg is defined as a twentieth century term for mechanical warfare involving tanks and aircraft. However, since it is widely applied to describe Grant's movements of May 1–17, 1863, I also use it. As we will see, the offensive quickly resulted in the elimination of the major supply line to Vicksburg, and the city's eventual siege and capture. Although he continuously augmented his command with additional troops, Grant conducted his blitzkrieg only with his original three corps, and while facing potentially greater odds against them. Keeping his command intact led to his eventual success.[32]

CHAPTER 5

GRANT'S BLITZKRIEG
MAY 1–17, 1863

When Ulysses S. Grant conducted what was to be labeled his blitzkrieg in May 1863, he reached the crux of his success. This action was probably the most outstanding campaign of the Civil War, and certainly one of the best in all of military history. In just over two weeks, he fought five battles and finally confronted his target all along: Vicksburg. Grant made three critical decisions during this time, Gen. Joseph E. Johnston one, and Lieut. Gen. John C. Pemberton one as well.

Grant Bypasses Vicksburg and Severs the Confederate Supply Line

Situation

While Sam Grant waited a few days for necessary supplies and troops to arrive at his location south of Vicksburg, he contemplated his next actions. Logically, he had positioned himself to make the final advance on the bastion of Vicksburg, and to make every effort to capture it. Of course, the Confederate high command recognized and expected the obvious, and the rebels prepared to defend their prize city controlling the Mississippi River. However, the Union commander began to visualize other possibilities to better plan for the ultimate thrust at and capture of the Hill City.[1]

Options

Certainly, one option was to immediately advance to Vicksburg and attempt to seize it. Yet another option was to temporarily bypass the city and sever its supply line. A third option would be to wait for further reinforcements before advancing.[2]

Option 1

Once Grant had finally positioned his command, or at least part of it, on the east bank of the Mississippi, the objective of the entire campaign was located only a matter of miles away. The sooner the Federal commander captured the city, the sooner he gained success. In addition, the sooner Grant took Vicksburg, the quicker the Mississippi River would be available for commercial (and military) traffic, while depriving the Confederacy of foodstuffs and men west of the river. However, to advance straight to the Confederate bastion would keep the Union army between the Mississippi River to the west and the Big Black River to the east—a potential place of entrapment. Within this rough triangle, the Confederates might prepare to assault the vulnerable Union command prior to reaching their target city. Until the Hill City could be completely surrounded, supplies could continue to flow into it via the Southern Railroad of Mississippi.[3]

Option 2

Although seemingly avoiding the objective of immediately capturing Vicksburg, severing the Southern Railroad also made sense. The railroad was an important supply line running some forty miles west from the major supply depot at Jackson, Mississippi, and the reduction in Confederate provisions if the line was cut would severely hamper the defense of Vicksburg. This option would require moving a fairly short distance to reach the railroad, and it might add to the Confederate high command's confusion as to where Grant would be maneuvering. The delay in severing the railroad likely would only last a few days, probably well worth the effort.[4]

Option 3

While waiting for Maj. Gen. William T. Sherman's corps to arrive, Grant could also order additional reinforcements. Although they would necessarily take days, if not weeks, to arrive, these soldiers would provide a force more capable of contending with whatever troops the Confederate high command mustered to protect Vicksburg. Motionless while awaiting reinforcements, the Union forces could be subject to an enemy assault.[5]

Decision

Grant chose to advance to the railroad and sever it, virtually eliminating supplies from Jackson to sustain the Confederate bastion at Vicksburg, and the Confederate forces trying to protect it.[6]

Results/Impact

On May 7 the Union commander began to advance his troops. Although Grant despised Maj. Gen. John McClernand's bombastic style and blatant political actions, he nonetheless placed the political general and his corps on the more exposed left flank, closest to a likely Confederate attack. Upon Sherman's arrival, that command would take up the march in the middle, while Grant's least experienced corps commander, Maj. Gen. James B. McPherson, was assigned the supposedly less vulnerable right flank. This force then moved inland, traveling northeast toward the Southern Railroad, which it aimed to sever somewhere between Bolton and Edwards Station. However, as we will see, this movement was interrupted before its conclusion. Ultimately, depriving Pemberton's Command of necessary supplies and ammunition led to the rebel general's surrender and the capture of Vicksburg.[7]

Alternate Scenario

Had Grant advanced directly toward Vicksburg as most everyone assumed he would, how might the campaign have changed? Challenged and confronted by those Confederate commands hastily brought together by Pemberton, the Union force might have been temporarily halted. Perhaps, somewhat trapped between the two rivers, the Union command would have had to wait for reinforcements, thus slowing its advance to the Hill City. The Federals might even have been defeated by additional Confederate reinforcements, considerably delaying the capture of Vicksburg.[8]

Sam Grant made another critical decision at this time that would assist his command in its movement against the supply line for Vicksburg, thereby allowing him more freedom of choice.

Grant Limits His Dependence on His Supply Line

Situation

One of the most promising ways to defeat an enemy is to attack him in his rear, which is even better than a flank attack. Of course, what is almost always in every army's rear is the supply line and depot. These are vulnerable to attack and must be protected. After U. S. Grant successfully won the Battle of Port Gibson, he and his command rested a few days, giving him time to reevaluate his next movements. Traditionally, an army must always protect its supply line as it advances into enemy territory, losing troops who must remain behind as guards.[9]

The disastrous raid on Holly Springs by Maj. Gen. Earl Van Dorn back in December 1862 had taught Sam Grant one valuable lesson. Cut off from his supply line and depot at that Mississippi town, the Union commander had discovered that, by ordering food to be rounded up for fifteen miles on both sides of the railroad he had been advancing on, he had much more of it than necessary to adequately supply his retreating army. Perhaps he might take advantage of that concept again?[10]

Options

Grant had three options for supplying his army as it moved farther into Confederate territory. He could establish a standard supply line with the necessary guards to ensure its protection. Alternatively, the commander might severely limit dependence on the line in order to provide more versatility, less concern, and a minimal target for Confederate attack. Finally, Grant could eliminate his supply line entirely for a brief period.[11]

Option 1

Any army needed to provide its troops with the required foodstuffs, clothing, ammunition, and other essentials in order to maintain order and efficiency while in the field, and especially within enemy territory. This measure was both necessary and critical for success, essentially considered part of the cost of doing business. Without all required provisions, Grant's soldiers would be unable to function, and the army would be forced to retreat back to where it could reacquire access to supplies. The downside of maintaining adequate stores was the requirement to continuously guard the supply line, which would require more and more soldiers as it was extended following the advancing army. Since Grant's supply depot would also be located in Confederate-held territory, it, too, would need significant manpower for protection.[12]

Option 2

Another option would be to place less emphasis on the Federals' supply line. Bringing the more important supplies with reinforcements marching to join Grant's already established command would temporarily work. Most provisions, including food and grain, ought to be available from the countryside, similar to the foodstuffs discovered along the railroad back in December. The one item that foraging would not provide was ammunition, which must be available for the troops.[13]

Option 3

If he completely severed all contact with his supply base, Grant could move in any direction as desired without concern to his rear. This ability would be short-lived, as the army could only survive on the supplies with it for a few days until goods such as ammunition began to run out.[14]

Decision

Grant decided about May 7, as his advance was getting underway, to select option 2, to limit his supply line to essentials only, other than food. Of course, ammunition would still have to be brought forward in order to keep the troops armed and ready for combat.[15]

Results/Impact

While a common misconception is that Sam Grant completely severed his supply line at this time, he did not. Yet he depended on it only for items he could not scavenge from the immediate countryside. By ordering arriving reinforcements to bring forward necessary supplies, Grant enabled his command to maneuver with much more latitude. Thus he focused on initially severing the Southern Railroad and eventually eliminating the Vicksburg supply depot, as we will see next. These actions significantly reduced the Confederates' ability to continue to fight.[16]

Alternate Scenario

Had Grant chosen the more traditional method of establishing and protecting a standard supply line, the Confederates might have severed it as the Union command advanced northeast. This might well have considerably changed his ability to maneuver as freely as he was able. The Federals' creation of a standard supply line might also have allowed the Confederates enough time to bring in additional reinforcements to stave off a final advance on Vicksburg, significantly altering the campaign.[17]

Grant Strikes at Jackson

Situation

As described above, the advance northeast began on May 7 with McClernand's corps on the left flank, Sherman's corps in the center, and McPherson's corps

Maj. Gen. James B. McPherson, USA
The Photographic History of the Civil War, Vol. X, p. 129.

on the less vulnerable right flank. Logically, the Confederates would wisely remain between the invading Union army and the Gibraltar of the West. The Union corps continued advancing toward the Southern Railroad with the goal of severing it, as mentioned above, somewhere between Edwards and Bolton, west of Jackson. While reinforced with some basic supplies and ammunition, the troops of the Union command were able to daily confiscate the majority of required foodstuffs as they continued to move deeper into Confederate territory.[18]

With minimal dispute McClernand's and Sherman's corps crossed Fourteenmile Creek, which roughly paralleled the railroad, on May 12, quickly dispersing Confederate defenders. However, McPherson, ordered by Grant to look for supplies at nearby Raymond, found something entirely different. On May 10 Pemberton ordered Brig. Gen. John Gregg, who had arrived at Jackson, to advance to the small town of Raymond to report on enemy movements. He marched his brigade there and encamped. On the twelfth Gregg observed dust from an approaching force and made what turned out to be a very poor decision. Convinced the advancing command was an enemy brigade, he decided to attack it with his three thousand men. In fact, this unknown force was the two lead divisions of McPherson's corps![19]

Gregg deployed his Seventh Texas along Fourteenmile Creek and sent

Brig. Gen. John Gregg, CSA.
The Photographic History of the Civil War, Vol. X, p. 157.

the Fiftieth Tennessee south at a right angle to the Raymond Road. He also located the Tenth/Thirtieth Tennessee behind the Fiftieth, and he placed the Third Tennessee near the cemetery to support both flanks. Additionally, Gregg brought forward Capt. Hiram Bledsoe's three-gun battery. As these troops opened fire on the initial elements of McPherson's lead divisions around 9:00 a.m., the corps commander first sent Brig. Gen. Elias Dennis's brigade forward over the right side of the road. This brigade was soon followed by Brig. Gen. John Smith's brigade. One by one, McPherson continued to send in brigades to counter the strong Confederate fire. Eventually it dawned on Gregg that the Union force he had stopped in its tracks was indeed much larger than he had first suspected. He then began ordering his regiments to retire from the field. McPherson claimed victory, but since he fed his brigades into the action piecemeal, they could only react to what they observed. McPherson won this small battle simply because of his overwhelming numbers, and not due to the good management of his command.[20]

Grant learned of the Battle of Raymond that evening, and it perturbed him. His constant fear of assault by Pemberton's command, and maybe Joe Johnston's as well, was that it would be launched on his left flank (McClernand's corps). This new attack on the Union right flank at Raymond challenged that thinking.[21]

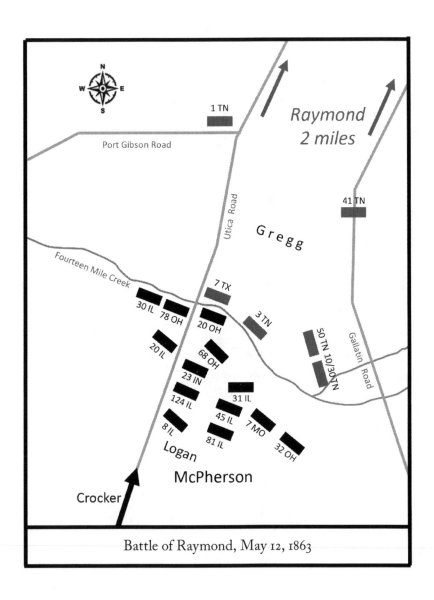

Battle of Raymond, May 12, 1863

Options

The Union commander suddenly faced choosing between two important courses of action. He could continue to advance as originally planned to sever the Southern Railroad. Alternatively, Grant could divert his command to maneuver to capture Jackson, apparently the source of additional Confederate units, potentially interfering with his advance on the railroad.[22]

Option 1

Grant's plan to sever the railroad initially confused Pemberton as to the Union commander's objective. Cutting this line still remained a viable objective, and it likely would be worth some casualties to achieve it. Once that task was complete, the Union army could then advance west to capture Vicksburg.[23]

Option 2

Reflecting on the assault on his right flank at Raymond by Confederates from Jackson, Grant realized that addressing this new source of enemy soldiers made sense. Rather than continuing to the railroad as previously planned, the Federals might secure their right flank. Additionally, the opportunity to advance to and capture Jackson would produce several positive results for Grant. Not only might he confront and defeat the Confederate force defending the Mississippi capital, but he could also eliminate the city as a source of supply for the Gibraltar of the West. Additionally, the source of supply would be eliminated as well. Finally, all communication from the east would cease.[24]

Decision

Sam Grant quickly revised his plan and decided to first move against Jackson per the reasoning of Option 2. A further deviation from his original strategy to move directly at Vicksburg after capturing Port Gibson, this course of action would cement his concept of eliminating virtually all supplies for Pemberton's troops, and potentially Johnston's as well.[25]

Results/Impact

Grant immediately issued orders to revise his corps' movements. Counting on Pemberton to remain at Edwards Station at least briefly, he ordered McClernand to take three of his divisions to Raymond to act as both the rear guard and the reserve for the advance to Jackson. McClernand's fourth division remained at Fourteenmile Creek awaiting Maj. Gen. Frank Blair's corps of Sherman's corps to arrive bringing supplies. Grant ordered McPherson's

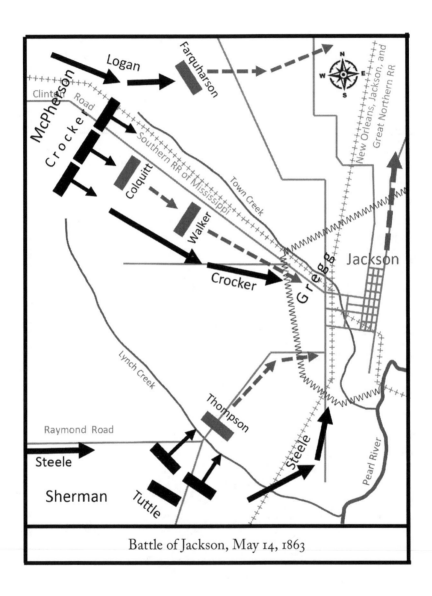

Battle of Jackson, May 14, 1863

corps to advance northeast to Clinton on the railroad, then advance southeast to Jackson. Meanwhile, Sherman's corps received orders to move directly to the capital from Raymond. At this time the Union commander would temporarily abandon his supply line and become totally mobile.[26]

After moving as ordered in rainy weather, and following brief fights by both Sherman's and McPherson's men, the Federals drove off the defending Confederates on May 14, Joseph Johnston's small command among them. Once the rebels left the city, the Union troops set about destroying everything of military importance, including a factory that employed women to make tent cloths. Sherman remained the next day and thoroughly destroyed many miles of railroad track radiating out from the capital. Jackson had now lost its importance as a supply and communications center for the duration of the war, certainly compromising Pemberton's ability to continue to fight.[27]

Alternate Scenario

Had Grant decided to continue north to sever the railroad and not advance east to Jackson, he would have potentially exposed his right flank and eventually his rear as he turned west following the railroad toward Vicksburg. Perhaps Johnston, emboldened by the opportunity, might have at least harassed the Union command as it advanced west, also saving the capital from destruction and continuing to provide communications from the east, especially Richmond.[28]

Johnston Determines He Cannot Assist Pemberton

Situation

By initiating this final movement against Vicksburg, U. S. Grant obviously made most of the critical decisions, with Pemberton and his commanders largely reacting to the Union commander. Finally an opportunity arose whereby a Confederate commander had the ability to address the latest Federal advance into Mississippi, aiming at the Hill City.

Back on November 24, 1862, Pres. Jefferson Davis had appointed Gen. Joseph E. Johnston to overall command of the Confederate Western Theater of operations. Johnston vacillated as to this huge responsibility. Specifically, he deemed it impossible to oversee two separate armies (Bragg's Army of Tennessee and Pemberton's Mississippi command). In order to understand this problem and follow the theater commander's line of thought, we must briefly examine his past relationship with Confederate president Jefferson Davis.[29]

Gen. Joseph E. Johnston, CSA. *The Photographic History of the Civil War*, Vol. X, p. 241.

Joseph E. Johnston was born at Cherry Grove, near Farmville, Virginia, on February 3, 1807, making him one of the older generals of the Civil War. He grew up in Abingdon, Virginia, located in the southwest part of the state, and attended the Abingdon Academy. As Joe desired a military education, his father, Judge Peter Johnston, convinced John C. Calhoun, then the secretary of war, to nominate him to the United States Military Academy at West Point, New York. Successfully admitted, the cadet graduated along with fellow first classman Robert E. Lee in 1829. Johnston fought in the Mexican-American War, where he was wounded, and he received two brevet promotions, the second to colonel. He eventually sparred with Secretary of War Jefferson Davis as to rank, and finally was confirmed as a colonel in 1860. Johnston's greatest success while a member of the US Army was promotion to quartermaster general on June 28, 1860, which entitled him the rank of brigadier general. However, this almost immediately caused problems for the new general officer.[30]

When the Civil War erupted shortly thereafter, Joseph Johnston decided to go with his state of Virginia. President Davis immediately promoted him to the rank of brigadier general, the highest then available, and placed him in command of the garrison at Harpers Ferry, Virginia. Reacting to orders, Johnston rushed his command to Manassas Junction soon after, where his last-minute arrival helped on-site commander P. G. T. Beauregard win the

First Battle of Bull Run, or First Manassas. Although outranking Beauregard, Johnston allowed the Louisianian to retain overall battlefield command.[31]

A bit of a rivalry already existed between Davis and Johnston from when the latter was vying for promotion in the US Army. During the second week in September 1861, the president published his list of newly authorized full generals in Confederate service, and Joe Johnston felt truly slighted. The new law authorized former Union army officers to hold their equivalent rank in the Confederate army. Johnston, the only brigadier, believed he should rank number one ahead of the other general officers, who were former colonels or majors. However, Davis considered Johnston a staff officer—which he was—who didn't outrank the others who were line officers. Although these categories were somewhat meaningless, since there were initially only five designated full general officers, Joseph Johnston went on a rampage, writing a fifteen-page letter to President Davis that pointed out the incredible wrong perpetrated against him. This was the beginning of a failing relationship between the two. After Johnston was severely wounded, Davis selected Gen. Robert E. Lee to command the Army of Northern Virginia during the Seven Days Battles. Following his recovery, General Johnston began to believe that the president was setting him up for failure when he was appointed to command the entire Western Theater.[32]

With this background of distrust, Johnston, although still recovering from his wounds, immediately traveled west to assume his new assignment. He attempted to pin down Davis as to which area of the Western Theater was the more important to protect: Tennessee, defended by Braxton Bragg's Army of Tennessee, or Vicksburg and Mississippi, defended by Pemberton's Army. Davis refused to specify one over the other, and Joe Johnston insisted that he could not safeguard both. Herein lay the problem. Further complicating the situation was the fact that Davis apparently had John Pemberton report directly to him in Richmond instead of communicating through Johnston. The Confederate president also meddled in departmental affairs, often leaving Johnston unaware of events within his sphere of command.[33]

One additional trait characterized Joseph Johnston: he feared nothing worse than failure itself. While out hunting with friends, he once refused to take a shot because he was afraid of missing his target. Trained at West Point in the Jominian way of battle, like most of his peers, he wished to consider attacking the enemy only when all facets of the operation were satisfactory. Unlike Ulysses S. Grant, who made do with what he had available and tried to confront his enemy, Johnston would wait for the correct circumstances before fighting. This was demonstrated time and time again later in the war during the Atlanta Campaign.[34]

However, General Johnston held one correct military strategy: with Grant targeting Vicksburg in May, the Confederacy could not afford to lose both the river bastion and the army defending it. The lesser of two evils would be to forfeit the garrison but salvage Pemberton's Army to fight another day. This would be Johnston's underlying view as he wrestled with how to stop Grant.[35]

On May 9 the Confederate high command, under the direction of Secretary of War James Seddon, ordered Johnston to proceed immediately to Mississippi and take command of the forces there. The department commander replied, "I shall go immediately although unfit for field service." Arriving in Jackson on May 13, Johnston discovered that he had about six thousand soldiers in the area. After sending orders to Pemberton he wired Richmond: "I am too late." Johnston had revealed his opinion of the situation.[36]

Options

Departmental commander Joseph Johnston now had two choices of action. He could maneuver against Grant and join with Pemberton's Army, or he could appear to do so, knowing that he was too late to save both Jackson and Vicksburg.[37]

Option 1

Johnston had no choice but to try and save Vicksburg from the Union army commanded by U. S. Grant, which was threatening Vicksburg and Jackson. He needed to somehow work in concert with Pemberton's Army in order to halt the Union progress. If Johnston couldn't prevent the eventual capture of the Confederate bastion, at least he could help save Pemberton's Army from becoming besieged, allowing it to fight another day. Of course, this potentially required combat on his part.[38]

Option 2

Johnston's other option was to go through the motions to help save Vicksburg from capture or prevent Pemberton from becoming besieged and captured. However, he would do so without committing to actually fight the invaders, instead relying on Pemberton to follow his orders.[39]

Decision

Sadly for the Confederacy, Joseph Johnston chose the second option. He continued to believe that, in general, he was too late to save the Hill City. He therefore maneuvered to keep his command safe while giving John Pemberton unrealistic orders to attack Grant or join forces with his small Confederate command.[40]

Results/Impact

As indicated, Johnston had become fixated on not losing Pemberton's Army in order to save Vicksburg. Pemberton received a series of orders to unite with Johnston's Command. However, on May 14, as the corps of Sherman and McPherson advanced to and captured the Mississippi capital of Jackson, Joseph Johnston retreated over twenty-five miles north toward Canton, directly away from Pemberton![41]

Meanwhile, as we will examine in discussion of the next critical decision, Pemberton, torn between orders from Johnston and orders from Davis, was left to confront Grant and his army. Skipping ahead to when Pemberton retreated into Vicksburg and was besieged, his only hope was either receiving assistance in breaking the attack, or escaping the city through the efforts of Johnston. These hopes were in vain. Johnston's failure to intervene led inexorably to Pemberton's eventual failure to save Vicksburg once besieged.[42]

Alternate Scenario

One can only imagine the potential difference a strong, aggressive Confederate commander, with characteristics such as those of Ulysses S. Grant, might have made by directly confronting the Union army attempting to capture Vicksburg. Against the wily Grant, any Confederate response would have had to be very calculated, correctly timed, and carefully carried out. Yet the rebels had several opportunities to assault parts of the Union army where they were vulnerable, such as at Raymond, Jackson, and after the loss of Jackson. While unlikely to eventually change the outcome of the loss of Vicksburg, such attacks might have prevented the loss of Pemberton's Army and significantly increased the number of Union casualties.[43]

Pemberton Mismanages His Defense of Vicksburg

Situation

This is an all-encompassing critical decision in that it consists of a trend of several failures by the Confederate commander to understand the situation and react, rather than one mistake in particular. While we will focus on the Battle of Champion Hill, John Pemberton somehow failed to comprehend that Grant was moving his army down the west side of the Mississippi.

Pemberton's attention was diverted to the raids of Grierson and Streight. Finally realizing Grant's intention after landing at Bruinsburg, Pemberton did not initially attempt to directly confront the Union commander as he maneuvered between Vicksburg and Jackson.[44]

In fairness to Lieutenant General Pemberton, President Davis placed him in a tough position, as both sides knew the Hill City was a vital target that would not be circumvented. Often ignoring how critical the situation was in Mississippi, the Confederate government in Richmond focused more on the Eastern Theater, where Gen. Robert E. Lee won a stunning victory at Chancellorsville in early May. Also, Davis made it perfectly clear to Pemberton that Vicksburg was to be protected at all costs; surrender of that city was not an option. Further, Davis apparently told Pemberton to report directly to him, bypassing the Western Theater commander Joseph Johnston. Thus Pemberton would eventually find himself often receiving two sets of conflicting orders from the two commanders. Soon, this forced him to obey one commander and disregard the other. Which one was correct?[45]

After Grant landed his army on Mississippi soil, Pemberton maneuvered his army to keep it between the Yankees and the Confederate bastion. As Joseph Johnston arrived at Jackson, he attempted some coordination but failed, as described above. Pemberton did send Gregg to Raymond, where he attacked McPherson's corps, which was en route to sever the Southern Railroad north of that location. After the Federals' successful small fight for and capture of Jackson, it became obvious to the Confederates that the Yankee force would next advance to its longtime objective of Vicksburg. This command would have to be stopped before it reached the Hill City, or else the Confederate force under Pemberton might have to retire to the fortifications protecting the Confederate citadel.[46]

After burning all buildings in Jackson that supported the Confederate military effort, and leaving Sherman's men to further destroy the railroads feeding into the capital, Ulysses S. Grant turned his back on the city and advanced west. Early on May 16, he placed McClernand's Thirteenth Corps on the advance westward toward his final goal. Brig. Gen. A. J. Smith's division and Maj. Gen. Francis P. Blair's division, which was temporarily loaned to McClernand, were on the Union left. Smith's and Blair's men were marching along the Raymond Road, which ran from that location gradually west-northwest to Edwards Station, a small town on the Southern Railroad. These troops were seeking what they believed to be the Confederate right flank. McClernand's center consisted of Brig. Gens. Peter J. Osterhaus's and Eugene A. Carr's divisions maneuvering along the Middle Road, which was roughly equidistant from the Raymond Road to its south and the Jackson

Road to its north. On the Jackson Road marched Brig. Gen. Alvin P. Hovey's division, supported by McPherson's two divisions commanded by Maj. Gen. John A. Logan and Brig. Gen. Marcellus M. Crocker.[47]

While the Union army had encountered some Confederate resistance as it advanced northeast to cut the Southern Railroad, and it had fought at Raymond and Jackson, Pemberton continued attempting to ascertain Grant's targets and react. The Confederate commander was finally beginning to listen to his generals, but he didn't seem to learn much. He had finally moved his headquarters from Jackson to Vicksburg on May 1 in order to remain more in touch with the Yankee movements. Pemberton was too late to defend Port Gibson, and then Grant stole a march on him by advancing toward the railroad, not directly to the Hill City. Nonetheless, Pemberton was inclined, due to past experience in South Carolina and to Davis's orders, to prioritize guarding the Confederate bastion rather than chasing after the invaders.[48]

Options

Disregarding Pemberton's previous failures to discern Grant's eventual movement down the west side of the Mississippi River, the Confederate commander faced a major decision concerning operations to save Vicksburg from capture. He could do his best to resist the Union commander's thrusts toward the Hill City by himself, or he could join forces with his theater commander Joseph Johnston.[49]

Option 1

Pemberton's orders from President Davis, as noted above, were to protect Vicksburg at all costs. His command size was comparable to his enemy's, and he perhaps might coerce Grant into attacking him at a place of his own choosing. Pemberton appeared to have already considered retreating into the environs of the Hill City a last resort in order to protect it for as long as possible.[50]

Option 2

Alternatively, per the continued requests of Johnston, Pemberton could join his force and attack Grant's command. However, the theater commander had made it clear that it was in the Confederacy's best interests not to lose Pemberton's Army as well if it were to lose the Hill City. However, Pemberton disagreed with Johnston, as per his orders from Richmond, all efforts must be made to preserve the bastion city.[51]

Decision

On May 15 Pemberton chose both options! He initially would attempt to confront the Army of the Tennessee somewhere east of Edwards Station, and then join forces with Johnston's Command, which had moved north of Jackson.[52]

Results/Impact

The immediate result of this "decision" was the Battle of Champion Hill, quickly followed by the Confederate disaster at the brief Battle of the Big Black River Bridge. This latter event essentially sealed the fate of the Confederate bastion at Vicksburg. Afterward, Pemberton's Army retreated into the lines at the city.[53]

As noted, on the fifteenth, after destroying anything of military value in the Mississippi state capital at Jackson, the Army of the Tennessee began advancing west toward its target of Vicksburg. After some dithering as to what to do, Pemberton also advanced east from Edwards Station. Unfortunately for him, he neglected to order a reconnaissance of the Raymond Road leading southeast from his location to Raymond. This road crossed Baker's Creek, which, due to rain, had washed away the bridge providing a crossing over it. After wasting several hours, Pemberton finally ordered his command to retrace its steps back to Edwards Station and then advance on the Jackson Road, where the bridge over Baker's Creek was still intact. Thus, after the day's marching (and the night's, for some troops), Pemberton's Army, less the two divisions guarding the Hill City, had actually only gained some four miles! The troops were positioned a few miles south of the railroad near Champion Hill, a slight rise in the terrain named for the local Sid Champion family, whose house was located just north of it.[54]

On the morning of May 16, the Yankees marching westward collided with units of Pemberton's Army around Champion Hill. Brig. Gen. A. J. Smith's division of McClernand's Thirteenth Corps was followed by Maj. Gen. Frank P. Blair's division of Sherman's Fifteenth Corps, temporarily assigned to McClernand. Smith's and Blair's divisions encountered Maj. Gen. W. W. Loring's division guarding the Raymond Road east of Baker's Creek. The Illinois politician's center, consisting of Osterhaus's and Carr's divisions, advanced on the Middle Road and halted in woods just east of the main intersection of the Jackson Road and the Middle Road. At this crossroads the Jackson Road turned west to Edwards Station. Leading south from the intersection was the Ratcliff Road, which ran southwest to the Raymond Road. This crossroads and Champion Hill northeast of it became the focal point of the upcoming battle. McClernand's final division, commanded by Hovey,

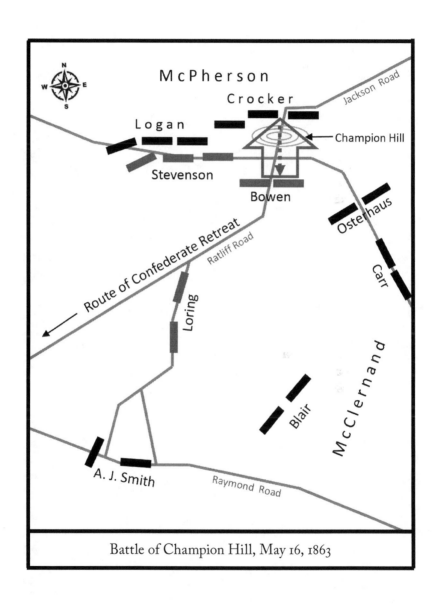

Battle of Champion Hill, May 16, 1863

marched west along the Jackson Road toward Champion Hill. Following him were McPherson's two divisions, commanded by Logan and Crocker. The Thirteenth Corps commander had been advised by Grant to advance cautiously. Grant also moved with the troops on the Jackson Road. According to author and historian Timothy Smith, with three divisions together on the Jackson Road, the Union commander had the potential to swing a great right hook on his enemy.[55]

Around 11:00 a.m. the two armies discovered each other, and preparations for battle commenced. Hovey's division formed up with his two brigades on and east of the Jackson Road, north of Champion Hill. To Hovey's right, Logan's brigades, commanded by Brig. Gens. John E. Smith, Mortimer D. Leggett, and John Stevenson, prepared to fight. Maj. Gen. Carter L. Stevenson observed the Federal force and notified Pemberton of its presence, then strove to confront the Yankees. Stevenson ordered Brig. Gen. Alfred Cumming's and Brig. Gen. Stephen D. Lee's men to attack the Federals moving up Champion Hill. On the right, Cumming, just west of the Jackson Road, was soon routed by Hovey's men. Lee's troops were later overrun by Leggett's and J. E. Smith's brigades. Meanwhile, Logan's third brigade, commanded by Stevenson, advanced west of the fighting around Champion Hill and blocked the Jackson Road, which provided a possible means of escape over Baker's Creek. The Confederate outlook was bleak.[56]

In desperation, Carter Stevenson sent his final brigade, commanded by Brig. Gen. Seth Barton, in haste to the northwest to confront the Yankee Stevenson's brigade. (Carter Stevenson's other brigade, commanded by Brig. Gen. Alexander W. Reynolds, had previously been sent just west of Baker's Creek on the Jackson Road to guard the four hundred Confederate wagons.) The rebel Stevenson also called for reinforcements from Pemberton, who immediately sent a messenger to order Brig. Gen. John Bowen and Maj. Gen. William W. Loring to provide support. In front of the messenger, Loring and his brigade commanders besmirched their commander and refused, citing their need to protect their positions! This stunning reaction was typical of Loring's longtime dissatisfaction with Pemberton. However, a second order to Bowen and Loring finally made them realize their presence was necessary, and they began moving northeast toward the active fighting.[57]

Bowen immediately advanced past Pemberton's headquarters at the Robert's house just south of the crossroads and headed into battle. His two brigades, commanded by Brig. Gen. Martin E. Green and Col. Francis M. Cockrell, consisted of combat veterans. Cockrell is generally regarded by historians as perhaps the finest brigade commander on either side of the Civil War. He was always ready to fight, and his highly trained command had injured many a Yankee. Arriving near the crossroads, Green's men moved into a line of battle just east of the Ratcliff Road with Cockrell's troops to their left, west of that road. These brigades then assaulted Hovey's two brigades under Brig. Gen. George F. McGinnis and Col. James R. Slack, already weary from battle. This counterattack was temporarily successful, pushing the Federals back over Champion Hill and recapturing some Confederate cannon.[58]

Carter Stevenson's remnants then rejoined the assault to the west. However, after some of the Yankees were routed, additional Union reinforcements began arriving. By about 3:00 p.m. Bowen's Command had pushed Hovey's men as far as humanly possible. Marcellus Crocker's division of McPherson's corps now advanced into the fray with three fresh brigades commanded by Cols. John B. Sanborn, Samuel Holmes, and George B. Boomer. They halted the Confederate offensive. This was the pinnacle of Confederate efforts. Complicating Bowen's assault was the fact that Carter Stevenson, for whatever reason, had ordered the ammunition wagons off the field of battle.[59]

Loring finally obeyed orders and began marching two of his brigades toward the crossroads. He left Brig. Gen. Lloyd Tilghman's Brigade to continue to defend the bridge over Baker's Creek on the Raymond Road. However, it was too late; the Union force around Champion Hill eventually overran the Confederates there, forcing them to retreat. Realizing the situation was now unacceptable, Pemberton ordered his command to commence retreating. With the Jackson Road now possessed by the Yankees, all remaining Confederate soldiers had to withdraw southwest to the Raymond Road and either cross Baker's Creek on the newly rebuilt bridge, or ford the receding waters. This allowed most of the surviving Confederate soldiers to escape. Tilghman and his brigade continued to hold off the Union divisions advancing west on the Raymond Road, but the general was killed while sighting a cannon.[60]

Most of the Confederate troops managed to fall back to and cross the bridge over Baker's Creek on the Raymond Road. However, Union soldiers, after crossing the same creek on the Jackson Road to the north, began advancing south, west of the creek, with the intention of capturing the escaping Confederates moving west on the Raymond Road. While most rebels did escape, these Yankees blocked Loring's Division from also slipping by. As a result, Loring moved his command south along the east side of Baker's Creek, away from the rest of Pemberton's Command. Eventually he found himself trapped on three sides, but, led by a local guide, Loring eventually made his escape. Disgusted with his commander, Loring unfortunately chose to march his command east to Jackson, rather than attempting to reunite with Pemberton's Army, and he later joined up with Joe Johnston and his small force. This decision left Pemberton in a terrible situation.[61]

Confederate losses in the Battle of Champion Hill were severe. Out of some 23,000 present, 381 irreplaceable Confederate soldiers were killed, 1,018 were wounded, and 2,441 were missing, likely captured, for a total of 3,840 casualties. Grant suffered a total of 2,441 casualties, identical to the number of Confederate captured and missing. Additionally, twenty-seven cannon were lost, as well as thousands of small arms. The Confederate commander retreated west to the last remaining natural obstacle before Vicksburg itself, the Big Black River. Quickly setting up a minimal defense with troops on the east side of the river, he awaited both Grant and Loring. As noted, Loring had simply disappeared, but not Grant. On May 17 the Federal soldiers quickly overran the poor Confederate defenses at the Battle of Big Black River (railroad) Bridge. This cost the defenders of Vicksburg another 1,800 soldiers and 18 more cannon. The dejected men of Pemberton's Army continued their retreat to the environs of the bastion at Vicksburg.[62]

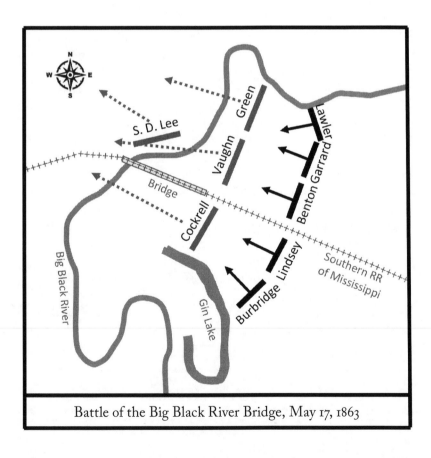

Battle of the Big Black River Bridge, May 17, 1863

Lieut. Gen. John Pemberton's mismanagement of the campaign so far, as well as his fumbling at the Battle of Champion Hill, set up the siege and eventual capture of the Gibraltar of the West. Poor work on the part of his staff, faulty use of intelligence, insufficient reconnaissance, and unsound tactics contributed to his monumental failure. Now bottled up in the trenches of Vicksburg, Pemberton was in the situation Johnston had so often warned about: he would eventually have to surrender both this so-important city and his army.[63]

Alternate Scenario

Pemberton's mindset was to defend Vicksburg, the task Jefferson Davis had assigned him. What would have happened if the general had decided to temporarily evade Grant's army and try to join up with Johnston's Command? Of course, Vicksburg would have quickly been captured by Grant, but the Confederacy would have not lost some thirty thousand critical soldiers. While the city might never have been recaptured, these men, joined with other Confederates, might have made a difference elsewhere.[64]

CHAPTER 6

ASSAULTS, SIEGE, AND SURRENDER
MAY 18–JULY 4, 1863

After the second defeat of Pemberton's Army in two days, the Confederates fell back inside their fortifications protecting Vicksburg from assault from the east. Maj. Gen. Ulysses S. Grant made the decision to attack first, rather than settle into a siege. With double failures to successfully assault, the siege began. When the Confederate commander eventually asked for terms of surrender, Grant made another significant decision to parole the Confederates, rather than send them to Union prisons.

Grant Assaults the Vicksburg Fortifications

Situation

After the twin defeats at the Battles of Champion Hill and Big Black River Bridge, Lieut. Gen. John C. Pemberton's remaining soldiers continued their retreat the last ten or so miles into the previously prepared fortifications surrounding Vicksburg on its east side. Although low on morale, those bedraggled men began to regain some semblance of order upon moving into this protective line. Maj. Gen. John H. Forney's and Maj. Gen. Martin L. Smith's divisions had remained in the city and were not worn out from the previous days of fighting. The Confederate commander quickly distributed his men along the eight-mile line anchored with both ends on the Mississippi River. This line consisted of large earthworks connected by rifle pits and parapets with places for artillery. Though it was already formidable, the defenders soon made the line even more so. As the Union corps spread out and covered the Confederate formation, Grant had a momentous decision to make: What to do next?[1]

Options

Doubting that the Confederates guarding the Hill City would immediately surrender, the Union commander must decide between two courses of action. His two choices were to assault the enemy fortifications or to begin siege operations.[2]

Option 1

Sam Grant's thinking at this time was that he had just defeated his opponents twice within a couple of days, meaning that their morale must be very poor, and that they must have less potential for strong resistance. If he assaulted the bastion city's fortification immediately, the defenders would have little time to strengthen their position. If he caught them off guard, the chances of Federal success would be good. Grant had momentum. Although he knew he would likely suffer significant casualties, an attack had the advantage of not requiring a lengthy siege, sparing Union troops weeks of toil and waiting for success.[3]

Option 2

If Grant simply decided to lay siege to the city, he would prevent the casualties incurred by an assault. The outcome of this choice would never really be in doubt; it would only be a matter of time before the besieged ran out of food or ammunition, forcing them to capitulate. The problem was that a siege would consume time, and Sam Grant did not like to waste time. He had already demonstrated that doing so was not part of his character. Unfortunately, especially earlier in his career, he had tended to be overconfident. Yet with adequate supplies now readily available, time was on Grant's side.[4]

Decision

Grant quickly decided to assault the Confederate works, ordering the attack to commence on May 19.[5]

Results/Impact

The Union commander ordered the assault to begin at 2:00 p.m. His three corps were positioned with Maj. Gen. William T. Sherman's on the north and northeast, Maj. Gen. James B. McPherson's on the east, north of the railroad, and Maj. Gen. John McClernand's south of the railroad. Sherman ordered Maj. Gen. Francis P. Blair's division, consisting of Brig. Gen. Hugh Ewing's, Col. Giles A. Smith's, and Col. Thomas K. Smith's brigades, to assault the Twenty-Seventh Louisiana Lunette and the Stockade Redan on the northeast corner of the Confederate line. McPherson assaulted the Confederate line in front of his position with several brigades, as did McClernand. Unfortunately, all of these Union attacks failed. The Confederates had regained some of their confidence and fought well. What would Grant try next?[6]

Grant's overriding concern had been to strike the Confederate formations before the defenders could get fully prepared to repel an assault, and while their morale was poor. He had hastily ordered the attacks on the nineteenth, before his troops were totally organized and in position. He had discovered the hard way that he was incorrect on both counts. Grant then reckoned that a better-organized, better-prepared assault might succeed. Therefore, he ordered another one for May 22.[7]

While preparing for the second assault Grant stabilized his supply line and brought in food and ammunition; he answered his troops' demands in doing so, as they had been campaigning the last week or so without a supply line. Union commanders also made more elaborate plans to better ensure success. The nature of the terrain had limited the previous assault to the three principal roads entering Vicksburg, which were the sites of especially strong fortifications precisely located to prevent the Yankees from forcing entry. Federal commanders organized storming parties that provided boards and other necessities to cross ditches and climb parapets. The various officers all set their watches to the same hour and minute. Grant ordered the attack, preceded by heavy artillery fire, to begin specifically at 10:00 a.m., and it did.[8]

Once again, Blair's division of Sherman's Fifteenth Corps assaulted along the Graveyard Road at the Stockade Redan. This time McPherson sent brigades on both sides of the Jackson Road defended by the Third Louisiana Redan. McClernand made three separate strikes on the Second Texas Lunette guarding the Baldwin Ferry Road, the Square Fort, and the Railroad Redoubt. Again, in spite of the more elaborate preparation, all attacks failed. Or had they?[9]

The political general John McClernand informed Grant that he had broken through and held two positions within the Confederate line. Around noon he requested help controlling these locations, and the Union commander told him to use his reserves. However, McClernand had already committed all of his command. He sent Grant three more requests for assistance. Grant told McPherson, whom he happened to be with, that he essentially didn't believe a word McClernand said. The corps commander replied that McClernand's requests could not be ignored until his claims were proved false, so Grant ordered reinforcements to McClernand, and McPherson to resume assaulting the Confederate line. Later, the generals discovered that McClernand had not actually captured any forts or positions on the Vicksburg line. At the same time, Union casualties in Sherman's corps from the second wave of assaults drove the overall Federal casualties up by 50 percent, with nothing to show for the loss of these men. Sam Grant was furious with McClernand and vowed to relieve him as soon as convenient. On June 19 some officers discovered that Sam's nemesis had issued a congratulatory order to his corps without permission, and it was published in some newspapers. Although this was a trivial misdeed, it nonetheless gave Grant the excuse to relieve McClernand. The Union commander quickly did so, replacing the now disgraced general with Maj. Gen. Edward O. C. Ord.[10]

Realizing that continuing to assault the Vicksburg fortifications simply would incur too many casualties, Grant was forced to order a siege of the Hill City. A siege typically began with a line of circumvallation, which was usually formed parallel to the enemy's own line and a few hundred yards from it. Fortified, it protected the siege troops from enemy fire, kept the besieged from breaking out of their fortress, and provided the base for covered advancement toward the enemy works. A line of contravallation was similar, except that it was located farther away. It also faced the opposite direction in order to protect the besieging force from assault or a relief effort by a force from outside it. Grant immediately went about establishing a line of circumvallation, and he eventually created one of contravallation. Rather than simply wait for the besieged command to surrender—and also to keep his men employed—Grant had the Federals dig approaches that gradually allowed them to advance to within only a few yards of the Confederate trenches. The previous Union assaults had failed due to the open terrain that had to be crossed, allowing the Confederates to fire many rounds at the attacking soldiers. However, after slowly advancing their entrenchments, the Federals would now cover only a few yards in their initial attack, and the besieged would be lucky to fire off a round before being overwhelmed.[11]

Often working at night where visibility was much reduced, Union troops rolled conical "saps" slowly forward in order to dig significantly protected trenches, eventually almost up to the Confederate line. During the day

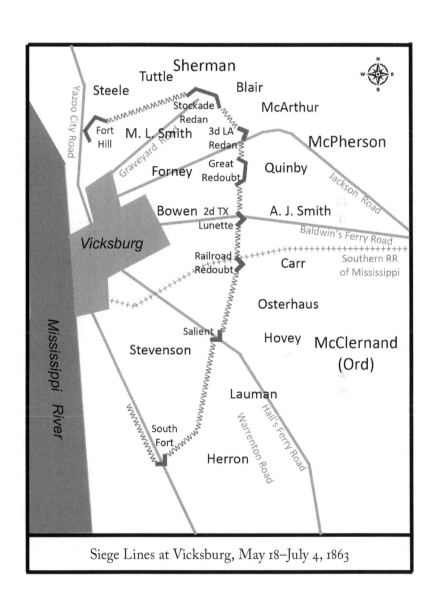

Siege Lines at Vicksburg, May 18–July 4, 1863

sharpshooters on both sides made life extremely dangerous for any soldier who exposed himself above a trench. Periodic Yankee battery fire forced all behind the Confederate line to seek safety. While stores dwindled behind the Confederate line, virtually unlimited supplies flowed to the Union troops via the Mississippi River and up the Yazoo River to Snyder's Bluff, northeast of Vicksburg and the Federal line. Grant kept additional reinforcements arriving to supplement his command, and he ordered Sherman to take part of his command and protect the Union rear.[12]

While the siege tightened around the Confederate line every day, Rear Adm. David D. Porter's Union navy also contributed to the Federal effort. Porter's gunboats and mortar rafts rained shot and shell daily on the Gibraltar of the West. Both citizens and Confederate soldiers suffered under the constant hours of bombardment. Although relatively few were killed by this means, the barrage added more misery to their already pitiful days. Many citizens created dugouts in the loose soil where they were generally safe from naval fire.[13]

All Confederate eyes were on Gen. Joseph Johnston to rescue the army under siege and liberate Vicksburg. While the general maintained a fighting game face, in reality he had already written off any chance of engaging with Grant's army. In hindsight, and judging from his May 13 message to Richmond in which he declared: "I am too late," it appeared that Johnston never intended to attempt to either confront the Union army or rescue the trapped Confederates. He did send several messages to Pemberton in an attempt to persuade him to escape, but this was most likely to give the appearance of doing something.[14]

As June passed into July, the Union army had dug its way to several places mere yards from the Confederate fortifications. Overall, the Federals were much closer to the enemy than they had been when the initial assaults of May 19 and 22 began. Mines were dug under the defenders' line, loaded with black powder, and set off on June 25 and July 2 with no major damage. By then the chance of success for a Federal assault was significantly higher. Grant's earlier critical decision to attack the Vicksburg fortifications had failed, resulting in the only other option he had, by default, which was establishing the siege. However, Grant ordered another assault for July 6, but circumstances described below made that decision moot. In fact, the siege guaranteed the eventual surrender of the Gibraltar of the West.[15]

Grant Paroles the Confederate Prisoners

Situation

The situation within Vicksburg had grown grimmer. Food and ammunition were low in supply, although the situation was not yet desperate. Pemberton reduced rations and cautioned against the use of ammunition except as necessary. But the soldiers' morale continued to fall, as well as their physical strength. By July 1, Pemberton knew he was running out of time. On June 28, he received an unsigned letter from "Many Soldiers," some of whom complained about the lack of food, contending that he must surrender if he couldn't supply more. On the first, Pemberton queried his division commanders as to whether to try to escape or surrender. All agreed that a successful escape was unlikely. The Confederate commander held a council of war on the night of July 2.[16]

At the council of war, the division commanders and Pemberton reviewed three possibilities. They could try to escape from the city, or they could continue to await Johnston for relief, or they could surrender. The officers dismissed the possibility of escape as the men were too weak, largely from the lack of a good diet. Also, they agreed that they were unlikely to receive any help from Joe Johnston. This realistically left only one course of action, eliminating the choice of surrender as a critical decision; as the rebels had no choice, capitulation was inevitable. Pemberton and his division leaders agreed to seek possible terms of surrender from the Union commander.[17]

Lieut. Gen. John Pemberton composed a letter to Grant on July 3 suggesting an armistice "with a view to arranging terms for the capitulation of Vicksburg." He proposed a selection of commissioners from both sides to establish the conditions of surrender. The letter was carried to the Union side under flags of truce by Brig. Gen. John Bowen, who had been a friend of U. S. Grant's in the past. Unfortunately for the Confederates, the Union commander reverted to both his initials and his past stance at Fort Donelson, demanding "unconditional surrender," although he indicated that he would treat the besieged with respect.[18]

When Bowen returned to headquarters, he hinted to Pemberton that Grant wished to meet with him. Therefore, at about 3:00 p.m., Pemberton, Bowen, and one of his aides, Lieut. Col. Louis M. Montgomery, crossed over the lines to near Union headquarters, where they met Sam Grant. Pemberton quickly ascertained that Grant had not requested the meeting. Bowen knew that Pemberton would reject the Union terms, so he had implied that each commander wished to speak with the other in order to set up a meeting. Of course, Pemberton refused the offered conditions. Yet Grant, knowing the Confederates would not be ready to capitulate if their food supply was adequate, allowed talks to continue. While the two commanders chatted about past service in the prewar army, Bowen and Montgomery discussed possible terms of surrender with Brig. Gen. Andrew J. Smith and Maj. Gen. James B. McPherson. Agreeing on a set of terms, around 10:00 p.m. the Union commander sent the final stipulations across the lines.[19]

Options

Part of the agreement caused Grant to make a critical decision about the fate of some thirty thousand surrendering Confederates. He could either send the prisoners north to prison camps already established, or he could parole these soldiers.[20]

Option 1

While the rebel surrender was certainly a great victory for both the Union and Grant, the loss of about thirty thousand irreplaceable soldiers was a serious blow to the Confederacy. Standard protocol was to ship these men off to established Union prisoner-of-war camps, where they would await their exchange or the war's conclusion. This movement would require a tremendous amount of coordination and logistical support, a detriment to the exchange. Transporting the prisoners up the Mississippi River initially by steamboat would require multiple trips back and forth by all available riverboats. The vessels would thus be unavailable for other uses, including supplying the huge Union force at and around Vicksburg. Grant remembered how troublesome it was dealing with the thousands of prisoners he had captured at Fort Donelson. Moving an even larger number of them after the surrender at Vicksburg would certainly overwhelm the whole transportation system of the Union.[21]

Option 2

Rather than assuming custody of all of these enemy soldiers, Grant could simply release them on parole. Theoretically, all of these men would remain out of further fighting until properly exchanged. Another factor that would be a significant advantage to paroling these prisoners was that many would likely immediately desert in order to go home, having little or no confidence in the Confederacy, and having endured enough of soldiering. Therefore, they would spread their lack of assurance in the future of the South while further depleting the strength of one of the Confederacy's larger armies. Also favoring this choice was the fact that the Confederacy did not presently have anywhere near the same number of Union prisoners to exchange.[22]

Decision

As part of the terms of surrender, Grant quickly chose to parole the captured besiegers.[23]

Results/Impact

Each Confederate officer and enlisted man was required to sign an individual parole, with a copy retained for each side. The Union commander assigned McPherson to find presses, print the paroles, and see that they were properly signed. Once these documents were signed and issued, the Confederates could leave. The officers were allowed to retain their side arms and one horse each, while the enlisted were able to leave with only their clothing. The theory was that the paroled soldiers would march to a designated location to await exchange, but, as noted above, Grant and his men assumed that many would desert, and many did.[24]

Because steamboats were not needed to remove the prisoners and take them north, these transports were immediately available to assist the Union commander with his next priorities. Likewise, the locations housing Confederate prisoners would not require additional space, guards, etc. This saved the Union countless thousands of dollars and untold man-hours![25]

As agreed to, on the morning of the Fourth of July the Confederates displayed white flags of surrender, marched out and stacked their arms and flags, and marched back into the city. The Union army moved into the Hill City and quickly raised the Stars and Stripes over the county courthouse. The Federals shared rations with their captors, and the parole process began, extending over about a week. Those Confederates who refused to sign paroles—around seven hundred men—were transferred north to prisons. Vicksburg was firmly in Union hands. As President Lincoln famously declared, "The Father of Waters again goes unvexed to the sea."[26]

CHAPTER 7

AFTERMATH
AND CONCLUSIONS

Maj. Gen. Ulysses S. Grant's victory at Vicksburg truly electrified the Union! Many believed that this was the death knell of the Confederacy. As the Confederate surrender at Vicksburg occurred at the same time as the defeat of Gen. Robert E. Lee's Army of Northern Virginia at Gettysburg, Union morale soared. Largely unnoticed, Maj. Gen. William S. Rosecrans's Tullahoma Campaign forced Gen. Braxton Bragg's Army of Tennessee back to Chattanooga, setting up the Battles of Chickamauga and Chattanooga.[1]

Capitulation at Vicksburg cost the South a large number of soldiers and a staggering amount of military equipment. On July 4, Pemberton ultimately surrendered to Grant 29,491 soldiers, along with 172 guns, some 50,000 small arms, 600,000 rounds of ammunition, 58,000 pounds of black powder, 38,000 artillery shells, and 350,000 percussion caps. Additionally, the Confederate commander relinquished 38,668 pounds of bacon, 5,000 bushels of peas, 51,241 pounds of rice, 92,234 pounds of sugar, and 428,000 pounds of salt. Since March 29, Grant suffered 10,142 casualties, while the Confederates incurred 9,091 casualties (plus those surrendered). The total number of prisoners captured during the Vicksburg Campaign was 30,638, an astonishing number![2]

Unsurprisingly, seven of the seventeen critical decisions were operational, while five were tactical. Two were personnel related, two were organizational, and one was logistical. Since Ulysses Grant was the aggressor, he made the vast majority of the critical decisions, forcing John Pemberton to react as best he could. As previously noted, reacting to critical decisions generally does not involve additional critical decisions, as the responding commander usually has little choice as to what action he must take.[3]

Students and historians of the Civil War often enjoy delineating the turning point or points of the conflict. By some definitions, the turning point of a war is when a specific action becomes the first of a series of events that inexorably result in the conquering of the enemy. Others believe that there can be a series of crucial moments, possibly on both sides, that eventually influence a war's outcome. For many students, historians, and members of the general public, the Battle of Gettysburg is perhaps the most generally accepted turning point of the Civil War. Federals and Confederates suffered a combined fifty thousand casualties in this largest battle of the war, a point that certainly must be considered. The Army of the Potomac defeated Lee's Army of Northern Virginia for the first time, forcing it back to Virginia. From that point on, Lee had no recourse but to generally fight on the defense. However, until Grant (yes, Grant) eventually forced Lee to surrender at Appomattox Court House after enduring a 292-day siege around Petersburg, no real change in territory or loss of armies occurred as a result of the Battle of Gettysburg.[4]

The capture of Vicksburg not only opened the Mississippi River for the Union all the way to New Orleans, but it also cut off nearly one-third of the Confederacy from the rest of the seceded nation. At least temporarily, the city's fall also removed some thirty thousand Confederate soldiers from the war. This certainly was significant military success, as well as a tremendous psychological boost to the Union citizenry! Yet in terms of ending the war, the Tullahoma Campaign, lasting just over a week, coinciding with Gettysburg and Vicksburg, and resulting in loss of only some six hundred Yankees, eventually set up the Battles of Chickamauga and Chattanooga. From there, the 1864 Atlanta Campaign resulted in the capture of that city, setting up Sherman's March to the Sea, his march through the Carolinas, and the surrender of most of the rest of the Confederate soldiers.[5]

On July 11 the paroled prisoners, led by Pemberton, left their place of besiegement and moved east to Enterprise, Mississippi, where they briefly halted to wait out their thirty-day parole period. They then departed and trudged to Demopolis, Alabama, where most received furloughs, many not to return.[6]

As noted above, while the process of paroling the Confederate defenders continued, besieged Port Hudson, the final Confederate choke point in the Mississippi River, unsurprisingly surrendered on July 9 upon learning of the fall of Vicksburg. Clear passage along the length of the river was finally available. Grant, still concerned about the possibility of Johnston's or some other commander's intent to interfere with his army, ordered his trusted subordinate Maj. Gen. William T. Sherman to once again march to Jackson and continue the destruction of any military supplies and resources, especially the railroads. Taking the Ninth, Thirteenth, and Fifteenth Corps with him, he marched once again to the capital.[7]

On June 28 Johnston had advanced west of Jackson with four divisions, possibly more for show than with any serious intent to confront the Union army. He stated his intentions thus: "[I will] make such close and careful examination of the enemy's lines as might enable me to estimate the probability of our being able to break them. . . . There is no hope of saving the place by raising the siege." By July 8 Johnston had quickly retreated back to Jackson and dug in. Confronting the Confederate commander, Sherman wisely decided not to order a direct assault, but exchanged artillery barrages instead. After failing to cut Sherman's supply line, and becoming duly impressed with the superior Federal artillery, Johnston evacuated Jackson on July 16, retreating east. The Union command pursued him to Brandon, where it wreaked havoc on the city. Sherman finally decided he had caused enough destruction and returned to Vicksburg, first taking time to add to the ruination of Jackson.[8]

While Sherman stayed busy, Grant did not. He proposed shifting toward Mobile in order to capture that important military location, but Halleck refused to allow that movement to occur. Therefore, Sam Grant found himself back on the defensive, a situation eerily similar to the one he'd been in a year previous. Also the same was the way in which his army soon found itself depleted. Grant was ordered to send some four thousand men to Maj. Gen. Nathaniel Banks at Port Hudson, which had surrendered on July 9, finally freeing the Mississippi River from Confederate control. The Union commander returned the Ninth Corps to Kentucky, and he sent another five thousand men to Maj. Gen. John Schofield in Missouri. The reinforcements to Schofield were to help confront Maj. Gen. Sterling Price, who was once again attempting to regain Missouri for the Confederacy. Grant was also directed to send a brigade to Natchez in order to provide a permanent garrison there. Finally, he received orders to cooperate with his nemesis Banks by providing him with Maj. Gen. E. O. C. Ord's Thirteenth Corps. As Grant indicated in his *Personal Memoirs*, "All of these movements came to naught."[9]

Because of Rosecrans's invasion of Tennessee and Georgia, on September 13 Halleck ordered Grant to send all available troops to support that effort. Ultimately, Grant dispatched four divisions commanded by Sherman. However, by the time these men were underway, Gen. Braxton Bragg's Army of Tennessee had defeated Rosecrans at the Battle of Chickamauga, and the

Union army was under something of a siege in Chattanooga. Finally realizing the need for a theater commander, Pres. Abraham Lincoln consolidated three western departments into the Military Division of the Mississippi, with Sam Grant as commander.[10]

Grant quickly moved to Chattanooga to take overall command and re-move the Federals from their predicament. He then replaced Rosecrans with Maj. Gen. George H. Thomas. Arriving in Chattanooga on October 23, Grant immediately went to work relieving the supply problem by establish-ing the Cracker Line, initially proposed by Rosecrans. In the meantime, he waited for the arrival of Sherman and his troops, who were marching by foot. Augmented by the Eleventh and Twelfth Corps, sent from the Army of the Potomac, Grant began planning to break out from the semi siege. As the Union force in Chattanooga grew with the arrival of Sherman's divisions, Bragg continued to reduce his command by sending parts of it away, ostensi-bly to provide assistance elsewhere.[11]

Beginning on November 24, Grant ordered assaults on Lookout Moun-tain and Missionary Ridge surrounding Chattanooga. Sherman let the Union commander down for once, failing to capture the north end of Missionary Ridge. However, troops under Maj. Gen. Joseph Hooker did seize control of Lookout Mountain, while Thomas's command actually climbed up Mission-ary Ridge, routing the Confederate defenders. Grant had successfully won his third campaign![12]

With the most important railroad crossroads of Chattanooga then safely in Union control, Grant began to plan for an invasion of Georgia. However, he would not lead it. Lincoln had finally concluded that he needed an ag-gressive general-in-chief to simultaneously direct the actions of all the Union armies. The president logically chose Sam Grant, his most successful general to date, and he revived through Congress the rank of lieutenant general to give the new general-in-chief full authority to command. The promotion was effective February 29, 1864, and Grant traveled to Washington, DC, to accept it on March 9 and meet the president for the first time.[13]

Of course, this resulted in a change of plans. Grant decided it would be best for him to remain east and accompany the Army of the Potomac, still commanded by Maj. Gen. George Meade, as he confronted Gen. Robert E. Lee. This required a new commander for the Military Division of the Mis-sissippi, and Grant immediately received approval to place Sherman in that position. So it was Sherman who directed what came to be known as the Atlanta Campaign. While other commands failed in their assignments, in-cluding Grant's own, Sherman's was to be the only one that gained success. Maj. Gen. Benjamin Butler failed to capture Richmond, Mag. Gen. Franz

Sigel could not gain control of the Shenandoah Valley, Banks conducted the disastrous Red River Campaign, and Grant wound up conducting a long term siege around Petersburg.[14]

Sherman immediately went about strengthening his supply line, the Western and Atlantic Railroad. In early May 1864, he began his advance to Dalton, Georgia, simultaneously with the launch of the other commands toward their objectives. Sherman turned Gen. Joseph E. Johnston out of his garrison at Dalton, fought him at the Battle of Resaca, and outflanked the Confederate commander, eventually leaving the railroad in yet another flanking maneuver. Unsuccessfully outflanking Johnston while fighting the "Hell-Hole" Battles of New Hope Church, Pickett's Mill, and Dallas in late May, Sherman ordered a direct assault against the center of Johnston's Kennesaw Mountain line. This assault failed, leading to more flanking. After Johnston retreated across the Chattahoochee River, just north of Atlanta, President Davis gave up hope that this general would ever halt the Federal invasion. Therefore, he replaced Johnston with temporary general John B. Hood. Hood went on the offensive, fighting but losing the Battles of Peachtree Creek, Atlanta, Ezra Church, and finally Jonesboro. After Sherman severed and destroyed the railroads supplying Atlanta, Hood abandoned the city late on September 1. The next day, the mayor surrendered it to the Union.[15]

After conducting a series of maneuvers trying to confront Hood's much-reduced army, Sherman decided to refocus his attention. He let Hood lead his small Army of Tennessee north to eventual defeats at the Battles of Franklin and Nashville, Tennessee, essentially rendering the Army of Tennessee ineffective. Refitting in Atlanta, Sherman carried out his (in)famous March to the Sea from mid-November, ultimately presenting Savannah, Georgia, to President Lincoln as a Christmas present. After further refitting, Sherman advanced his two wings north through South and North Carolina, destroying anything of military value, while planning to join Grant's army and help relieve the siege around Petersburg.[16]

In spite of Lee's tenacity, Grant finally broke the siege of Petersburg on April 2, leading to the Confederate commander's short attempt to escape. After a series of maneuvers, Grant cornered Lee near Appomattox Court House, and the rebel general surrendered his Army of Northern Virginia on April 9, 1865. Shortly thereafter, General Johnston, once again in command, surrendered the ragtag army attempting to confront Sherman as he marched through the Carolinas. The Civil War was, for all intents and purposes, over. Many of these actions to end the war built on Grant's victory at Vicksburg.[17]

Serving after the war as commander of the US Army, Ulysses S. Grant would be elected president of the United States, serving from 1869 to 1877.

He died of throat cancer in 1885, almost immediately after completing his memoirs.[18]

John Pemberton's career after the loss of Vicksburg took a much different path. Per the terms of his parole, he supposedly reported to his commander Gen. Joseph E. Johnston after the surrender. Received warmly by Johnston, Pemberton coldly saluted and walked away; the two would never again meet. After marching to Enterprise, Mississippi, with only a small part of his command, Pemberton joined his family in Demopolis. Thoroughly rejected by Confederate troops designated to serve under his command, he resigned his commission as lieutenant general in 1864 and reverted to the rank of lieutenant colonel, subsequently commanding the Richmond Defense Battalion of Artillery. After the war he returned home to manage his farm and become a teacher. Still generally reviled by Southerners, Pemberton died on July 13, 1881.[19]

There is perhaps no better way to sum up the Vicksburg Campaign than to quote Pres. Abraham Lincoln's message to Grant following his successful campaign.

> To Major-General Grant:
>
> My dear general: I do not remember that you and I ever met personally. I write this now as a grateful acknowledgment for the almost inestimable Service you have done the country. I wish to say a word further. When you first reached the vicinity of Vicksburg, I thought you should do what you finally did—march the troops across the neck, run the batteries with the transports, and thus go below; and I never had any faith, except in a general hope that you knew better than I, that the Yazoo Pass expedition and the like could succeed. When you got below and took Port Gibson, Grand Gulf, and the vicinity, I thought you should go down the river and join General Banks; and when you turned northward east of the Big Black, I feared it was a mistake. I now wish to make the personal acknowledgment that you were right and I was wrong.
>
> Yours very truly,
> A. Lincoln.[20]

These are truly words of praise and thanks from Grant's commander in chief!

APPENDIX I

DRIVING TOUR OF THE CRITICAL DECISIONS OF THE VICKSBURG CAMPAIGN

The driving tour of the critical decisions of the Vicksburg Campaign begins at the Vicksburg National Military Park visitor center, located at 3201 Clay Street, east of downtown Vicksburg, Mississippi. From Interstate 20, take Exit 3, Clay Street and follow the signs. For days and hours of operation, check www.NPS.gov/vick, call 601-636-0583, or email the park via the website just noted. The visitor center is a great place to get oriented, receive answers to your questions, and use the restrooms as necessary. The driving tour of some of the preserved Confederate and Union fortifications begins here as well, and it is definitely worthwhile for better understanding the challenges the Union army faced in order to capture the city.

Please remember that this is a tour of the sites where some of the critical decisions were made, and it presents the reader with a sense of the terrain and distances involved. It is not a tour of the various battlefields per se, although it certainly features parts of them. You may deviate from this route at your discretion to examine other parts of the battlefields and locations. Because this is not a tour of the campaign, we will generally drive on modern roads for ease of travel, rather than try to follow the 1863 roadways. Be aware that there are many other locations pertinent to the Vicksburg Campaign that are not

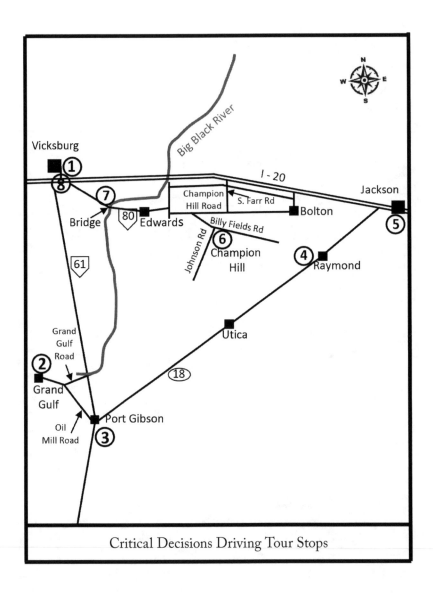

Critical Decisions Driving Tour Stops

part of this journey. Also, please follow commonsense safety procedures such as not reading while driving and having passengers do so instead, parking safely out of traffic, and keeping aware of your surroundings.

The driving tour creates a circle that covers a little over 150 miles and typically can be done in one day, subject to your own pace. There are eight stops on the tour, essentially chronological, with Stops 1 and 8 at the Vicksburg National Military Park. Several of the critical decisions were made elsewhere, such as Washington, DC, and Richmond, Virginia. Because of the impracticality of including these on the travel route, we will address them below at the first stop. If desired, the Stop 8 decisions can also be covered at Stop 1.

Stop 1—Vicksburg National Military Park Visitor Center

Critical Decisions: (1) Davis Appoints Pemberton Commander of the Department of Mississippi and Eastern Louisiana, (2) Stanton Appoints Grant to Command the Department of the Tennessee, (3) Davis Fails to Unify Command of the Mississippi River, (4) Grant Decides to Advance South into Mississippi, (5) Confederates Strike Grant's Supply Line, (6) Grant Advances down the West Side of the Mississippi, (7) Porter Agrees to Run Past Vicksburg

Davis Appoints Pemberton Commander of the Department of Mississippi and Eastern Louisiana

On September 30, 1862, Confederate president Jefferson Davis appointed Maj. Gen. John C. Pemberton to command the Department of Mississippi and Eastern Louisiana. Because Maj. Gen. Earl Van Dorn was operating within this department and was senior to Pemberton, Davis promoted Pemberton to the rank of lieutenant general on October 10 to establish him as the unequivocal commander of the department.

Message from Gen. Samuel Cooper to Maj. Gen. John C. Pemberton

SPECIAL ORDERS NO. 73 ADJT. AND INSP. GENERAL'S OFFICE
Richmond, Va., October 1, 1862
The State of Mississippi and that part of Louisiana east of the Mississippi River is constituted a separate military department, the command of which is assigned to Maj. Gen. John C. Pemberton.

By order:
S. Cooper
Adjutant and Inspector General[1]

Pemberton had virtually no combat experience, but he was a friend of President Davis's. Due to misunderstanding and inability to please the leading residents of Charleston, the president decided to replace him with Gen. P. G. T. Beauregard. This would eventually force a fairly inexperienced Pemberton to confront a proven combat commander in Ulysses S. Grant. Adding further confusion was the fact that Pemberton reported directly to Davis, bypassing theater commander Gen. Joseph E. Johnston. Eventually disregarding orders from Johnston, Pemberton inferred that his number one mission was to protect Vicksburg at all costs.

Stanton Appoints Grant to Command the Department of the Tennessee

After Pres. Abraham Lincoln appointed Maj. Gen. Henry W. Halleck general-in-chief of the Union armies, command of the Department of the Tennessee remained open. The Washington high command decided to place Grant in that position, making it official on October 25, 1862.

Message from L. Thomas to Maj. Gen. Ulysses S. Grant

GENERAL ORDERS NO. 159 WAR DEPARTMENT, ADJT. GEN.'S OFFICE
Washington, October 16, 1862
I. The Department of the Tennessee will include Cairo, Fort Henry, and Fort Donelson,
II. Northern Mississippi, and the portions of Kentucky and Tennessee west of the Tennessee River.
Maj. Gen. U. S. Grant is assigned to the command of the Department of The Tennessee.

By order of the Secretary of War:
L. Thomas
Adjutant-General[2]

Grant had previously captured Forts Henry and Donelson, and had won the Battle of Shiloh on the second day of fighting, after being caught by surprise the day before. He exhibited a tenacity to go after his enemy, and the upcoming Vicksburg Campaign demonstrated this trait to both military and civilians alike. His selection for command of this department eventually led to perhaps the most brilliant campaign of the Civil War, ultimately freeing the Mississippi River for Union commerce, dividing the Confederacy almost in two, and providing a decisive turning point in the war.

Davis Fails to Unify Command of the Mississippi River

To protect all areas of the Confederacy, President Davis divided it into a series of departments, each commanded by a general with a supporting army or organization of troops. For ease of drawing boundaries, Davis often relied on natural geographical ones, such as state lines and rivers. Because the Mississippi River easily defined boundaries for individual departments, he often used it to mark borders. Unfortunately, assigning the east bank of the river to one department meant that another separate department controlled the west bank. A Union army marching down the Mississippi River needed to be confronted before it possibly crossed over to the other side, as Grant eventually did. This required cooperation that individual department commanders rarely gave.

Defending against the enemy moving up or down a river logically required both banks of the river to be within the same department, nominally led by one officer. This arrangement eliminated any coordination problems. Unfortunately, in this situation only Jefferson Davis could either redefine the departmental boundaries or order cooperation between departmental commanders. While originally ordering collaboration between Pemberton's and Lieut. Gen. Edmund Kirby Smith's departments, the Confederacy's secretary of war did so on behalf of the president without verifying the decision with him. This resulted in the secretary's resignation. Therefore, Davis thought that he could not give the same order without losing face. Thus he then believed that he could only request cooperation, allowing Grant's army to advance virtually unmolested down the river.

Message from President Davis
to Lieut. Gen. John C. Pemberton

Lieutenant General Pemberton: Richmond, May 7, [1863]—11:30 p.m.

... To hold both Vicksburg and Port Hudson is necessary to a connection with Trans-Mississippi. You may expect whatever is in my power to do.
Jefferson Davis[3]

Needless to say, the president failed to officially order cooperation between Pemberton and Kirby Smith. In fairness to Pemberton, Davis handicapped his ability to confront the Union advance, and the president must share some of the blame for Grant's ultimately successful maneuvering to capture Vicksburg.

Interestingly, back in October Ulysses Grant recognized the problem with commands divided by the Mississippi River.

Message from Maj. Gen. Ulysses S. Grant to Maj. Gen. Henry W. Halleck

Headquarters Department of the Tennessee
Jackson, Tenn., October 26, 1862
General H. W. Halleck, Washington, D.C.

... I am now holding New Madrid with detachments from troops of this command, which General Curtis has assumed control over, and coolly informs me that he cannot spare them. I would respectfully suggest that both banks of the river be under one command.

U. S .Grant
Major-General[4]

Grant Decides to Advance South into Mississippi

As soon as Stanton appointed Grant to command the Department of the Tennessee, he made plans to advance toward his objective: the capture of the citadel of Vicksburg. He began organizing his new command to carry out a campaign to realize his goal.

Message from Maj. Gen. Ulysses S. Grant
to Maj. Gen. Henry W. Halleck

Jackson, Tenn., November 2,—11:00 a.m.

I have commenced a movement on Grand Junction with three divisions from Corinth and two from Bolivar. Will leave here To-morrow evening and take command in person. If found practicable, I will go on to Holly Springs, and maybe Grenada, completing railroad and telegraph as I go. Bolivar has been threatened for some days, but it may be a feint to cover a retreat.

U. S. Grant
Major-General, Commanding

Maj. Gen. H. W. HALLECK, General-in-Chief[5]

He further explained his plan of action.

Narrative of Maj. Gen. Ulysses S. Grant, USA,
Commanding Army of the Tennessee

Personal Memoirs

Vicksburg was important to the enemy because it occupied the first high ground coming close to the river below Memphis. From there a railroad runs east, connecting with other roads leading to all points of the Southern States. A railroad also starts from the opposite side of the river, extending west as far as Shreveport, Louisiana. Vicksburg was the only channel, at the time of the events of which this chapter treats, connecting the parts of the Confederacy divided by the Mississippi. So long as it was held by the enemy, the free navigation of the river was prevented. Hence its importance. Points on the river between Vicksburg and Port Hudson were held as dependencies; but their fall was sure to follow the capture of the former place.

The Campaign against Vicksburg commenced on the 2nd of November as indicated in a dispatch to the general-in-chief.[6]

In his memoirs, Grant continued to explain his plan to advance toward Vicksburg while dealing with Maj. Gen. John McClernand:

At this stage of the campaign against Vicksburg I was very much disturbed by newspaper rumors that General McClernand was to have a separate and independent command within mine, to operate against Vicksburg by way of the Mississippi River. Two commanders on the same field are always one too many, and in this case I did not think the general selected had either the experience or the qualifications to fit him for so important a position. I feared for the safety of the troops intrusted to him, especially as he was to raise new levies, raw troops, to execute so important a trust. But on the 12th I received a dispatch from General Halleck saying that I had command of all the troops sent to my department and authorizing me to fight the enemy where I pleased. The next day my cavalry was in Holly Springs, and the enemy fell back south of the Tallahatchie.

Holly Springs I selected for my depot of supplies and munitions of war, all of which at that time came by rail from Columbus, Kentucky, except the few stores collected about La Grange and Grand Junction. This was a long line (increasing in length as we moved south) to maintain in an enemy's country. On the 15th of November, while I was still at Holly Springs, I sent word to Sherman to meet me at Columbus. We were but 47 miles apart, yet the most expeditious way for us to meet was for me to take the rail to Columbus and Sherman a steamer for the same place. At that meeting, besides talking over my general plans I gave him his orders to join me with two divisions and to march them down the Mississippi Central Railroad if he could. Sherman, who was always prompt, was up by the 29th to Cottage Hill, ten miles north of Oxford. He brought three divisions with him, leaving a garrison of only four regiments of infantry, a couple of pieces of artillery and a small detachment of cavalry. Further reinforcements he knew were on their way from the north to Memphis. . . .

. . . During the delay at Oxford in repairing railroads I learned that an expedition down the Mississippi was inevitable and, desiring to have a competent commander in charge, I ordered Sherman on the 8th of December back to Memphis to take charge. The following were his orders:

Headquarters 13th Army Corps,
Department of the Tennessee, Oxford, Mississippi, December 8, 1862
Maj. Gen. W. T. Sherman, Commanding Right Wing

You will proceed, with as little delay as possible to Memphis, Tennessee, taking with you one division of your present command. On your arrival at Memphis you will assume command of all of the troops there, and that portion of General Curtis's forces at present east of the Mississippi River, and organize them into brigades and divisions in your own army. As soon as possible move with them down the river to the vicinity of Vicksburg, and with the co-operation of the gunboat fleet under command of Flag-officer Porter proceed to the reduction of that place in such manner as circumstances, and your own judgement, might dictate.

The amount of rations, forage, land transportation, etc., necessary to take, will be left entirely with yourself. The Quartermaster at Saint Louis will be instructed to send you transportation for 30,000 men; should you still find yourself deficient, your quartermaster will be authorized to make up the deficiency from such transports as may come into the port of Memphis.

Inform me at the earliest practicable day of the time when you will embark, and such plans as may then be matured. I will hold the forces here in readiness to co-operate with you in such manner as the movements of the enemy may make necessary.

Leave the District of Memphis in the command of an efficient officer, and with a garrison of four regiments of infantry, the siege guns, and whatever cavalry may be there.

U. S. Grant
Major-General.[7]

Thus the Union commander had set up a two-pronged approach to hopefully confuse the Confederates as to exactly who was advancing where. This critical decision to advance down the Mississippi Central Railroad, with a diversion conducted by Sherman, was about to be countermanded.

Confederates Strike Grant's Supply Line

As noted above by Grant himself, the farther south he advanced, the longer and more tenuous his supply line became. Still a believer in the Jominian theory that an army must have a solid supply line in order to function, the Union commander continued to worry about maintaining this route. He had every reason to do so, for the Confederates were already scheming to sever it.

And indeed they were. Several cavalry colonels suggested that a select force of troopers commanded by Maj. Gen. Earl Van Dorn might sever the Union supply line, significantly altering Grant's plans. When this suggestion was approved, Van Dorn quickly formed a command of three cavalry brigades and rode into action. Carefully maneuvering his men, he approached Holly Springs undetected early on the morning of December 20. The rebels immediately wreaked havoc on the Union supply depot while rendering Grant's supply line inoperable.

Report of Maj. Gen. Earl Van Dorn to Lieut. Gen. John C. Pemberton

Holly Springs, Miss., December 20, 1862

I surprised the enemy at this place at daylight this morning; burned up all the quartermaster's stores, cotton, etc.—an immense amount; burned up many trains; took in a great many arms and about 1,500 prisoners. I presume the value of stores would amount to $1,500,000. I move on to Davis' Mills at once. Morgan attacked Jackson day before yesterday. . . .

Earl Van Dorn
Major-General[8]

Narrative of Maj. Gen. Ulysses S. Grant, USA, Commanding Army of the Tennessee

Personal Memoirs

On the 20th General Van Dorn appeared at Holly Springs, my secondary base of supplies, captured the garrison of 1,500 men commanded by Colonel Murphy, of the 8th Wisconsin regiment, and destroyed all our munitions of war, food and forage. The capture was a disgraceful one to the officer commanding but not to the troops under him. At the same time Forrest got on our line of railroad between Jackson, Tennessee, and Columbus, Kentucky, doing much damage to it. This cut me off from all communication with the north for more than a week, and it was more than two weeks before rations or forage could be issued from stores obtained in the regular way.

This demonstrated the impossibility of maintaining so long a line of road over which to draw supplies for an army moving in an enemy's country. I determined, therefore, to abandon my campaign into the interior with Columbus as a base, and returned to La Grange and Grand Junction destroying the road to my front and repairing the road to Memphis, making the Mississippi river the line over which to draw supplies. Pemberton was falling back at the same time.[9]

Sherman, initially unaware of Grant's new predicament, had moved down the Mississippi and up the Yazoo River northeast of Vicksburg. On December 29 he ordered an assault at Chickasaw Bayou. The terrain heavily favored the Confederate defenders, pinning down the Yankees. Sherman finally realized that his plan and assaults were failures; the Federals lost 1,776 men compared with just a couple of hundred Confederate casualties. The commander's report of the battle was succinct.

Report of Maj. Gen. William T. Sherman, USA, Commanding Second Corps, Army of the Mississippi

On board Forrest Queen, January 5, 1863

Sir: Communication with General Grant seems cut off; at all events so difficult that much time will be consumed in my transmitting through him an official account of our movements on the river that I have concluded to send you direct—

First. A copy of my official report.

Second. A map of the ground and water before Vicksburg.

Third. My official instructions to commanders of divisions.

Fourth. Copy of my orders for the assault and battle.

I reached Vicksburg at the time appointed, landed, assaulted, and failed.[10]

Grant now needed to devise a new plan to capture the Hill City.

Grant Advances down the West Side of the Mississippi

Ulysses Grant knew he had to reevaluate his methodology of capturing Vicksburg. There were multiple options to consider or reconsider.

Narrative of Maj. Gen. Ulysses S. Grant, USA, Commanding Army of the Tennessee

Personal Memoirs

The real work of the campaign and siege of Vicksburg now began. The problem was to secure a footing upon dry ground on the east side of the river from which the troops could operate against Vicksburg. The Mississippi River, from Cairo south, runs through a rich alluvial valley of many miles in width, bound on the east by land running from eighty up to two or more hundred feet above the river. On the west side the highest land, except in a few places, is but little above the highest water. Through this valley the river meanders in a most tortuous way, varying in direction to all points of the compass. At places it runs to the very foot of the bluffs. After leaving Memphis, there are no such highlands coming to the water's edge on the east shore until Vicksburg is reached.

The intervening land is cut up by bayous filled from the river in high water—many of them navigable for steamers. All of them would be, except for overhanging trees, narrowness and tortuous course, making it impossible to turn the bends with vessels of any considerable length. Marching across this country in the face of an enemy was impossible; navigating it proved equally impracticable. The strategical way according to the rule, therefore, would have been to go back to Memphis; establish that as a base of supplies; fortify it so that the storehouses could be held by a small garrison, and move from there along the line of railroad, repairing as we advanced, to the Yallabusha [Yalobusha], or to Jackson, Mississippi. At this time the North had become very much discouraged. Many strong Union men believed that the war must prove a failure. The elections of 1862 had gone against the party which was for the prosecution of the war to save the Union if it took the last man and the last dollar. Voluntary enlistments had ceased throughout the greater part of the North, and the draft had been resorted to fill up our ranks. It was my judgement at the time that to make a backward movement as long as that from Vicksburg to Memphis, would be interpreted, by many of those yet full of hope for the preservation of the Union, as a defeat, and that the draft would be resisted, desertions ensue and the power to capture and punish deserters lost. There was nothing left to be done but to *go forward to a decisive victory.* This was in my mind from the moment I took command in person at Young's Point.[11]

Grant tried four different schemes to somehow get behind Vicksburg, but they all failed. He apparently didn't have much confidence in any of them, but the attempts kept the soldiers and sailors occupied. The general realized that his only other choice was to bypass the Hill City by marching down the west side of the Mississippi.

Narrative of Maj. Gen. Ulysses S. Grant, USA, Commanding Army of the Tennessee

Personal Memoirs

I had had in contemplation the whole winter the movement by land to a point below Vicksburg from which to operate, subject only to the possible but not expected success of some of the expedients resorted to for the purpose of giving us a different base. This could not be undertaken until the waters receded.[12]

Porter Agrees to Run Past Vicksburg

Once Grant positioned his army south of Vicksburg on the west bank of the Mississippi River, he had no choice but to rely on the US Navy to help ferry his men across the river to the east bank. The navy's cooperation was crucial to carrying out his latest plan of operation.

Narrative of Maj. Gen. Ulysses S. Grant, USA, Commanding Army of the Tennessee

Personal Memoirs

I did not therefore communicate this plan, even to an officer of my staff, until it was necessary to make preparations for the start. My recollection is that Admiral Porter was the first one to whom I mentioned it. The co-operation of the navy was absolutely essential to the success (even to the contemplation) of such an enterprise. I had no more authority to command Porter than he had to command me. It was necessary to have part of his fleet below Vicksburg if the troops went there. Steamers to use as ferries were also essential. The navy was the only escort and protection for these steamers, all of which in getting below had to run about fourteen miles of batteries. Porter fell into the plan at once, and suggested that he had better superintend the preparation of the steamers selected to run the batteries, as sailors would probably understand the work better than soldiers. I was glad to accept his proposition, not only because I admitted his argument, but because it would enable me to keep from the enemy a little longer our designs.[13]

Porter successfully ran past the Vicksburg and Grand Gulf batteries twice, on April 16 and 22, positioning the gunboats and steamers for the eventual ferrying of Grant's army from the west bank to the east bank of the Mississippi River. Once on the east side of the Mississippi, the Union commander next executed his blitzkrieg.

Stop 2 on the driving tour is Grand Gulf Military Monument Park, about 34.0 miles south-southwest of Vicksburg. Exit Vicksburg National Military Park by turning southeast onto Clay Street, and drive about a half mile to the entrance to I-20. Turn right (southwest) onto I-20, and drive about 3.0 miles to Exit 1B, US 61S. Take the exit, and continue southwest just under 23.0 miles to the intersection with Grand Gulf Road. Turn right (west), and continue 7.3 miles to Grand Gulf Military Monument Park. Continue to the visitor center, park, and enter if the site is open. For information and days and hours of operation, call 601-437-5911, or visit the park's website at www.grandgulfpark.ms.gov. At your discretion, visit the batteries and small town.

Stop 2—Grand Gulf Military Monument Park

Critical Decisions: (7) Porter Agrees to Run Past Vicksburg, (8) Grant Decides to Land at Bruinsburg.

Porter Agrees to Run Past Vicksburg

On March 29, McClernand's corps of the Union army began marching down the west bank of the Mississippi River below Vicksburg, soon followed by

McPherson's corps, and eventually Sherman's. As described above, Porter twice ran the batteries of Vicksburg to transport the Union army across the Mississippi to the east bank. Grand Gulf contained two batteries of large-caliber cannon, Forts Cobun and Wade, plus some field artillery, and any Union boats attempting to run by it faced a challenge.

Grant Decides to Land at Bruinsburg

Grant determined that Grand Gulf, downriver from Vicksburg, was a good candidate to be his ferry destination. Not only could he land his troops there, but he could also establish a supply base easily accessible to Union steamers. Therefore, Grant requested Admiral Porter to reduce the batteries defending that location and inhibiting Federal travel on the river.

Narrative of Maj. Gen. Ulysses S. Grant, USA, Commanding Army of the Tennessee

Personal Memoirs

At 8 o'clock a.m., 29th, Porter made the attack with his entire strength present, eight gunboats. For nearly five and a half hours the attack was kept up without silencing a single gun of the enemy. All this time McClernand's 10,000 men were huddled together on the transports in the stream ready to attempt a landing if signalled [*sic*]. I occupied a tug from which I could see the effect of the battle on both sides, within range of the enemy's guns; but a small tug, without armament, was not calculated to attract the fire of the batteries while they were being assailed themselves. About half-past one the fleet withdrew, seeing their efforts were entirely unavailing. The enemy ceased fire as soon as we withdrew. I immediately signalled [*sic*] the Admiral and went aboard his ship. The navy lost in this engagement eighteen killed and fifty-six wounded. A large proportion of these were of the crew of the flagship, and most of these from a single shell which penetrated the ship's side and exploded between decks where the men were working their guns. The sight of the mangled and dying men which met my eye as I boarded the ship was sickening.

Grand Gulf is on a high bluff where the river runs at the very foot of it. It is as defensible upon its front as Vicksburg and, at that time, would have been just as impossible to capture by a front attack. I therefore requested Porter to run the batteries with his fleet that night, and to take charge of the transports, all of which would be wanted below.[14]

Report of Brig. Gen. John S. Bowen, CSA, Commanding Bowen's Division, Army of Vicksburg

Grand Gulf, April 29, 1863

Six gunboats, averaging ten guns, have been bombarding my batteries terrifically since 7 a.m. They pass and repass the batteries at the closest ranges. I cannot tell the effect of our shots. Six transports in sight, loaded with troops, but stationary. My loss as yet only 2 killed. The batteries, especially the lower ones, are badly torn to pieces. I cannot tell the result, but think that reinforcements would hardly reach me time to aid in the defense if they attempt to land.

After six hours and a half of continued firing, the gunboats have retired. They fired about 3,000 shot and shell, temporarily disabling one gun. Our loss is 3 killed and 12 or 15 wounded. Apparently we injured two of their boats; damage unknown. Col. William Wade, of the artillery, one of the bravest and best in my command, was killed at his post. The men behaved like veterans (as they are), and are now hard at work preparing for another attack.[15]

Report of Lieut. Gen. John C. Pemberton, CSA, Commanding Army of Vicksburg

Jackson, April 29, 1863

Six gunboats, averaging ten guns each, opened a terrific fire upon our batteries at Grand Gulf at 7 a.m., and continued without intermission six hours and a half, when they withdrew. Several boats apparently damaged, one, disabled, lying on Louisiana shore below. Our loss, 3 killed, including Colonel [William] Wade, General Bowen's chief of artillery; 12 or 15 wounded. Repairs are being made, expecting a renewal of attack to-morrow. Transports loaded with troops in sight, but inactive.[16]

Obviously, the Union landing location on the east bank of the Mississippi River needed to change.

Report of Maj. Gen. Ulysses S. Grant, USA, Commanding Army of the Tennessee

This determined me again to run the enemy's batteries, turn his position by effecting a landing, at Rodney or at Bruinsburg, between Grand Gulf and Rodney. Accordingly, orders were immediately given for the troops to debark at Hard Times, La., and march across to the point immediately below Grand Gulf.

At dark the gunboats again engaged the batteries, and all the transports run by, receiving but two or three shots in the passage, and these without injury. I had sometime previously ordered a reconnaissance to a point opposite Bruinsburg, to ascertain, if possible, from persons in the neighborhood the character of the road leading to the highlands back of Bruinsburg. During the night I learned from a negro man that there was a good road from Bruinsburg to Port Gibson, which determined me to land there.

The work of ferrying the troops to Bruinsburg was commenced at daylight in the morning, the gunboats as well as the transports being used for the purpose.[17]

A large part of Grant's army was now safely below both the Vicksburg and Grand Gulf batteries. The general positioned himself to invade Mississippi once again, and close in on his objective, the Gibraltar of the West.

Stop 3 on the driving tour is about 8.0 miles south-southeast at the city of Port Gibson. Depart from the south end of the park, and drive about 3.8 miles on Grand Gulf Road to the intersection with Oil Mill Road on the right. Turn right (south), and continue 2.6 miles to where the road becomes Anthony Street. Continue another 0.8 mile until Anthony Street becomes Orange Street; the change will occur as you pass by the Claiborne County Courthouse on the left (north). Continue a block to the intersection with US 61 / Church Street, and carefully park. You are in downtown Port Gibson. Feel free to explore the third-oldest city in Mississippi if you have the time and inclination.

Stop 3—Port Gibson

Critical Decisions: (8) Grant Decides to Land at Bruinsburg, (9) Grierson's Raid and Other Diversions Confuse Pemberton, (10) Grant Decides Not to Support Banks, (11) Grant Bypasses Vicksburg and Severs the Confederate Supply Line, (12) Grant Limits His Dependence on His Supply Line

Grant Decides to Land at Bruinsburg

Bowen's batteries at Grand Gulf had successfully resisted Porter's assault with his gunboats, forcing Grant to find another location on the east bank of the Mississippi River to disembark his army. As noted above, a local Black man suggested Bruinsburg, north of Rodney. If a landing here was successful, it would save Union soldiers time spent traveling the longer distance to Port Gibson. Grant ordered the command ferried to Bruinsburg, and the troops met no resistance on coming ashore. Incidentally, this movement of some twenty-two thousand men was one of the largest amphibious landing of soldiers until World War II! In addition to Col. Benjamin H. Grierson's raid, Sherman's fake Snyder's Bluff demonstration also kept Pemberton from sending an adequate force to contest the landing of Federal troops on the east bank, as the rebels' attention was diverted. The Union commander did fear the public might take a negative view of a demonstration by Sherman to fool the Confederates, considering it as some sort of a retreat.

Message from Maj. Gen. Ulysses S. Grant to Maj. Gen. William T. Sherman

Smith's Plantation, La., April 27, 1863

Maj. Gen. William T. Sherman, Cmdg. Fifteenth Corps:

If you think it advisable, you may make a reconnaissance of Hayne's Bluff, taking as much force and as many steamers as you like. Admiral Porter told me that he would instruct Captain Breese to do as you asked him with his fleet. The effect of a heavy demonstration in that direction would be good so far as the enemy are concerned, but I am loth to order it, because it would be so hard to make our own troops understand that only a demonstration was intended, and our people at home would characterize it as a repulse. I therefore leave it to you whether to make such a demonstration. If made at all, I advise that you publish your order beforehand, stating that a reconnaissance in force was to be made for the purpose of calling off the enemy's attention from our movements south of Vicksburg, and not without any expectation of attacking. I shall probably move on Grand Gulf tomorrow.

U. S. Grant[18]

Message from Maj. Gen. William T. Sherman to Maj. Gen. Ulysses S. Grant

Milliken's Bend, April 28, 1863

Major-General Grant, Comdg. Dept. of the Tennessee, Carthage:

Dear General: I received your letter of the 27th last night, and early this morning went to see Captain Breese, and agreed with him as to the demonstration on Haynes' Bluff the moment the Choctaw arrives. She was at Memphis last Saturday, and should be here to-day. I will take ten steamers and ten regiments, and go up the Yazoo as close to Haynes' as possible without putting the transports under the rifled guns of the enemy. We will make as strong a demonstration as possible. The troops will all understand the purpose, and will not be hurt by the repulse. The people of the country must find out the truth as best they can; it is none of their business. You are engaged in a hazardous enterprise, and, for good reasons, wish to divert attention; that is sufficient to me, and it shall be done. I will be ready at daylight, and shall embark the men the moment Captain Breese notifies me he is ready.[19]

Once Sherman finished his demonstration, Grant ordered him to move back south and join up with the Army of the Tennessee.

Meanwhile, Grant had successfully conducted the landing of McClernand's Thirteenth Corps and part of McPherson's Seventeenth Corps at Bruinsburg. The site of Disharoon's plantation, which was the location of Grant's command on the west bank of the Mississippi, shifted later on and is now in the middle of the river. Bruinsburg is now privately owned and inaccessible to the public. That is the reason for discussing the crossing at this location.

Report of Maj. Gen. Ulysses S. Grant, USA, Commanding Army of the Tennessee

The work of ferrying the troops to Bruinsburg was commenced at daylight in the morning, the gunboats as well as transports being used for the purpose.

As soon as the Thirteenth Army Corps was landed, and could draw three day's rations to put in haversacks (no wagons were allowed to cross until the troops were all over), they were started on the road to Port Gibson. I deemed it a matter of vast importance that the highlands should be reached without resistance. The Seventeenth Corps followed as rapidly as it could be put across the river.

About 2 o'clock, May 1, the advance of the enemy was met 8 miles from Bruinsburg, on the road to Port Gibson. He was forced to fall back, but as it was dark, he was not pursued far until daylight.

Early on the morning of the 1st, I went out accompanied by members of my staff, and found McClernand with his corps engaging the enemy about 4 miles from Port Gibson. At this point the roads branched in exactly opposite directions, both, however, leading to Port Gibson. The enemy had taken position on both branches, thus dividing, as he fell back, the pursuing forces. The nature of the ground in that part of the country is such that a very small force could retard the progress of a much larger one for many hours. The roads usually run on narrow, elevated ridges, with deep and impenetrable ravines on either side. On the right were the divisions of Hovey, Carr, and [A. J.] Smith, and on the left the division of Osterhaus of McClernand's corps. The three former succeeded in driving the enemy from position to position back toward Port Gibson steadily all day.[20]

While operations on the east bank of the Mississippi River were just getting underway, Sam Grant nonetheless had reason to be thankful.

Narrative of Maj. Gen. Ulysses S. Grant, USA, Commanding Army of the Tennessee

Personal Memoirs

The embarkation below Grand Gulf took place at De Shroon's, Louisiana, six miles above Bruinsburg, Mississippi. Early on the morning of the 30th of April McClernand's corps and one division of McPherson's corps were speedily landed.

When this was effected I felt a degree of relief scarcely ever equalled [*sic*] since. Vicksburg was not yet taken it is true, nor were its defenders demoralized by any of our previous moves. I was now in the enemy's country, with a vast river and the stronghold of Vicks-

> burg between me and my base of supplies. But I was on dry ground
> on the same side of the river with the enemy. All the campaigns,
> labors, hardships and exposures from the month of December pre-
> vious to this time that had been made and endured, were for the
> accomplishment of this one object.[21]

Soon the Union took possession of Port Gibson, where Grant regrouped.

Grierson's Raid and Other Diversions Confuse Pemberton

Grant's landing at least part of his command at Bruinsburg was a significant action, as just noted. Placing McClernand's corps and a division of
McPherson's corps on the east bank of the Mississippi River finally gave
Grant the opportunity to advance on Vicksburg, although, as we will see, he
ordered some detours prior to arriving there. What significantly aided this
movement was the comparative lack of opposition by the Confederates.

Brig. Gen. John Bowen was a proven brigade and division commander,
and he had kept his eye on the Union general's movement down the west side
of the Mississippi River. He sent many warnings to Pemberton, who seemed
to disregard them. While Bowen contested the Union army's advance to Port
Gibson as best he could, his force was no match for the number of Union
troops. Why was that? To a great degree, Col. Benjamin Grierson's cavalry
raid deep into Mississippi diverted Pemberton's attention away from Grant's
movements. A main target of his raid was the Southern Railroad at Newton
Station, located some sixty-five miles east of Jackson, which he severed on
April 24. Eventually Grierson and his worn out command arrived at Feder-
ally held Baton Rouge on May 2, after sixteen days in the saddle. Side raids
by small parts of his command also added to the Confederate confusion.
Additional raids by several other Union cavalry commands, and Sherman's
intentionally false movement on the Yazoo, also contributed to Pemberton's
confusion.

Because of these raids, Pemberton did not heed Bowen's warnings, which
led to this Confederate commander's inability to halt Grant's progress to Port
Gibson and beyond. Meeting no resistance upon landing, Grant regrouped
and supplied his men before beginning the movement inland to establish a
supply depot of sorts at the soon-to-be abandoned Grand Gulf. He certainly
appreciated Grierson's and the other commanders' efforts to keep the Confederates off balance and allow his initial landing to be unopposed.

Report of Maj. Gen. Ulysses S. Grant, USA,
Commanding Army of the Tennessee

Grand Gulf, Miss., May 6, 1863
Via Cairo, Il., May 8
Maj. Gen. H. W. Halleck
General-in-Chief

I learn that Colonel Grierson, with his cavalry, has been heard of; first about ten days ago, in northern Mississippi. He moved thence and struck the railroad 30 [actually 65] miles east of Jackson, at a point called Newton's Station. He then moved southward toward Enterprise, demanded the surrender of the place, and gave one hour's grace, during which General Loring arrived. He left at once, and moved toward Hazlehurst, on the New Orleans and Jackson Railroad. At this point he tore up the track; thence to Byhalia, 10 miles further south on the same road; thence eastward on the Natchez road, where he had a fight with Wirt Adams' cavalry. From this point he moved back, to the New Orleans and Jackson Railroad, to Brookhaven, 10 miles south of Byhalia. When last heard from, he was 3 miles from Summit, 10 miles south of the last-named point, supposed to be making his way to Baton Rouge. He has spread excitement throughout the State, destroying railroads, trestle-works, bridges, burning locomotives and railway stock, taking prisoners, and destroying stores of all kinds. To use the expression of my informant, "Grierson has knocked the heart out of the State."

U. S. Grant
Major-General, Commanding[22]

Narrative of Maj. Gen. Ulysses S. Grant, USA,
Commanding Army of the Tennessee

Personal Memoirs

It was at port Gibson I first heard through a Southern paper of the complete success of Colonel Grierson, who was making a raid through central Mississippi. He had started from La Grange April 17th with three regiments of about 1,700 men. On the 21st he detached Colonel Hatch with one regiment to destroy the railroad between Columbus and Macon and then return to La Grange. Hatch had a sharp fight with the enemy at Columbus and retreated along the railroad, destroying it at Okalona [*sic*] and Tupelo, and arriving in La Grange April 26. Grierson continued his movement with about 1,000 men, breaking the Vicksburg and Meridian railroad and the New Orleans and Jackson railroad, arriving at Baton Rouge May 2nd. This raid was of great importance, for Grierson had attracted the attention of the enemy from the main movement against Vicksburg.[23]

Grant Decides Not to Support Banks

Once established in Port Gibson, the Union commander took the opportunity to make several more critical decisions. One of the first was choosing not to send one of his corps to support Maj. Gen. Nathaniel Banks, who was attempting to capture the other Confederate bastion guarding the Mississippi River at Port Hudson. Banks outranked Grant, and the loss of one of Grant's corps would render his chances of success against Vicksburg much less likely. However, the Union high command expected his full cooperation to assist Banks. Nonetheless, Grant decided not to give it.

Report of Maj. Gen. Ulysses S. Grant, USA
Commanding Army of the Tennessee

About this I received a letter from General Banks, giving his position west of the Mississippi River, and stating that he could return to Baton Rouge by May 10; that by the reduction of Port Hudson he could join me with 12,000 men.

I learned about the same time that troops were expected at Jackson from the southern cities, with General Beauregard in command. To delay until May 10, and for the reduction of Port Hudson after that, the accession of 12,000 men would not leave me so strong as to move promptly with what I had. Information received from day to day of the movements of the enemy also impelled me to the course pursued.[24]

Grant divulged more of his thinking. He briefly traveled to Grand Gulf, which had been abandoned by the Confederates, and he cleaned up for the first time in a week.

Narrative of Maj. Gen. Ulysses S. Grant, USA, Commanding Army of the Tennessee

Personal Memoirs

While at Grand Gulf I heard from Banks, who was on the Red River, and who said that he could not be at Port Hudson before the 10th of May and then with only 15,000 men. Up to this time my intention had been to secure Grand Gulf as a base of supplies, detach McClernand's corps to Banks and co-operate with him in the reduction of Port Hudson.

The news from Banks forced upon me a different plan of campaign from the one intended. To wait for his co-operation would have detained me a least a month. The reinforcements would have not reached ten thousand men after deducting casualties and the necessary river guards at all high points close to the river for over three hundred miles. The enemy would have strengthened his position and been reinforced by more men than Banks could have brought. I therefore determined to move independently of Banks, cut loose from my base, destroy the Confederate force in rear of Vicksburg and invest or capture the city.[25]

This decision allowed Grant to soon begin his blitzkrieg, eventually resulting in the capture of the Hill City. By the time Halleck and Lincoln received notice of his decision not to cooperate with Banks, Sam Grant was well into his movements to cut off supplies and communication with Vicksburg. Then the two men could only hope for his success.

Grant Bypasses Vicksburg and Severs the Confederate Supply Line

While waiting for the rest of his command to arrive at Port Gibson, Grant contemplated his next move. Logically, he should advance directly to Vicksburg and fight the decisive battle for control of it. However, moving directly toward the city would place his army in a sort of triangle with the Mississippi River on his left and the Big Black River on his right. A Confederate force could attack his men from the north, keeping him boxed in. With no outlet, Grant's command could face decimation, if not capture.

Narrative of Maj. Gen. Ulysses S. Grant, USA, Commanding Army of the Tennessee

Personal Memoirs

After McPherson crossed the Big Black at Hankinson's ferry Vicksburg could have been approached and besieged by the south side. It is not probable, however, that Pemberton would have permitted a close besiegement. The broken nature of the ground would have enabled him to hold a strong defensible line from the [Mississippi] river south of the city to the Big Black [River], retaining possession of the railroad back to that point. It was my plan, therefore, to get to the railroad east of Vicksburg, and approach from that direction [east]. Accordingly, McPherson's troops that had crossed the Big Black were withdrawn and the movement east to Jackson commenced.[26]

Grant's new plan to initially bypass Vicksburg temporarily confused Pemberton. While the rebel officer eventually projected that the new advance was indeed to cut the Confederate railroad supply line from Jackson, he reacted too late. Grant advanced toward Edwards Station with McClernand's corps on the more vulnerable left, Sherman's in the center, and McPherson's on the presumed safer right.

Report of Maj. Gen. Ulysses S. Grant, USA Commanding Army of the Tennessee

On May 7, an advance was ordered, McPherson's corps [temporarily] keeping the road nearest the Big Black River, to Rocky Springs, McClernand's corps keeping the ridge road from Willow Springs, and Sherman following with his corps divided on the two roads. All the ferries were closely guarded until our troops were well advanced. It was my intention here to hug the Big Black River as closely as possible with McClernand's and Sherman's corps, and get them to the railroad at some place between Edwards Station and Bolton.[27]

All three corps continued to advance in the general direction of the all-important railroad that carried supplies from Jackson to Vicksburg.

Grant Limits His Dependence on His Supply Line

The final critical decision Grant made in or around Port Gibson was to limit his need for supplies shipped down the Mississippi, ferried across that river, and hauled by wagons or other vehicles to the Union army. Sam Grant had learned the previous December that his army could live largely off the land. Certain provisions were not readily attainable off the land, especially ammunition. Therefore, he ordered only the truly necessary items for his army, and these would move from Grand Gulf to his corps via vehicles captured and guarded by reinforcements en route to the Union troops.

One common misconception is that Grant cut his army off from resupply at this point. This is not true: while additional supplies were kept to a minimum, they continued to flow to his troops. Only for a few days after the capture of Jackson did the army operate virtually on its own to live off the land.

Narrative of Maj. Gen. Ulysses S. Grant, USA, Commanding Army of the Tennessee

Personal Memoirs

Even Sherman, who afterwards ignored bases of supplies other than what were afforded by the country while marching through four states of the Confederacy with an army more than twice as large as mine at this time, wrote me from Hankinson's ferry, advising me of the impossibility of supplying our army over a single road. He urged me to "stop all troops till your army is partially supplied with wagons, and then act as quick as possible; for this road will be jammed, as sure as life." To this I replied: "I do not calculate upon the possibility of supplying the army with full rations from Grand Gulf. I know it will be impossible without constructing additional roads. What I do expect is to get up what rations of hard bread, coffee and salt we can, and make the country furnish the balance." We started from Bruinsburg with an average of about two days' rations, and received no more from our own supplies for some days; abundance was found in the mean time. A delay would give the enemy time to reinforce and fortify.[28]

This lesser dependence on a supply line gave Grant much more flexibility to move as necessary while confusing Pemberton, who assumed that the Union commander would need a conventional supply line. Thus Grant continually outmaneuvered his enemy.

Stop 4, the Raymond Battlefield, is about 42.0 miles northeast of Port Gibson. Depart the intersection of Orange Street and Church Avenue / US 61, and head north for about 0.5 mile. At the intersection with MS 18, turn right. Continue east, then northeast on MS 18 about 42.0 miles to the gravel road entrance to the Raymond Battlefield on the left (northwest). Park, leave your vehicle, and view the battlefield and markers.

Stop 4—Raymond Battlefield

Critical Decision: (13) Grant Strikes at Jackson

The Union army advanced to the northeast generally in the direction of Edwards Station or Bolton, both located on the Southern Railroad of Mississippi. As previously noted, Grant, for all of his disdain for McClernand, left him and his corps on the left flank, the one more likely to be assaulted. Sherman's corps remained in the middle, while McPherson's advanced on the presumably less vulnerable right flank. That assumption was about to change.

While repositioning his command, Pemberton ordered Brig. Gen. John Gregg to bring his brigade up from southern Mississippi via railroad to Jackson. He arrived, and on May 11 Pemberton ordered him to the small town of Raymond, a dozen or so miles west-southwest of Jackson, to keep an eye on enemy movements. Early on the twelfth, Gregg deployed his brigade along Fourteenmile Creek, just southwest of Raymond, where the enemy was spotted. Gregg decided to attack, unaware of the size of McPherson's command. The assault caught McPherson by surprise, but he began feeding in regiments to confront this unknown opponent.

Report of Brig. Gen. John Gregg, CSA, Commanding Gregg's Brigade, Walker's Division, Army of Relief

At Camp in Madison County, Miss., May 20, 1863

While in camp 2 miles east of Jackson, Miss., at 3 a.m. on the 11th instant, I received a dispatch from the lieutenant-general commanding, directing me to move my brigade promptly to Raymond, and I was directed to use Wirt Adam's cavalry, at Raymond, for advanced pickets.

By 5 o'clock the entire brigade was on the march, and at 4 p.m. we were at camp near Raymond. Upon my arrival I found the people

---

in great consternation, being under the impression that the enemy were advancing from Port Gibson. I found none of Colonel Adam's cavalry except a single sergeant and 4 men. There was a small state company, under the command of Captain Hall, who were, as I was informed, scouting in the direction of Port Gibson. I immediately sent forward Sergeant Miles and 4 men to put themselves in communication with Captain Hall, and bring me what information of the enemy's movements could be obtained. I also placed strong infantry pickets on the road leading out southwardly and to the west.

. . . Early the next morning I was informed by couriers from Captain Hall that the enemy was advancing rapidly by the road from Utica. . . . I was unable to ascertain anything as to the strength of the enemy. A dispatch from the lieutenant-general commanding intimated that the purpose of the enemy was supposed to be an advance upon Edwards Depot, and I inferred from it that that it was possible that the force in front of me was a brigade on a marauding excursion.[29]

As McPherson's troops advanced to Fourteenmile Creek, Gregg's men opened fire, and the Battle of Raymond commenced. The corps commander fed troops in brigade by brigade, eventually overcoming the small Confederate force.

Report of Maj. Gen. James B. McPherson, USA, Commanding Seventeenth Corps, Army of the Tennessee

About 11 a.m., and within 2 miles of Raymond, we came upon the enemy, under the command of General Gregg, and 4,000 or 5,000 strong, judiciously posted, with two batteries of artillery so placed as to sweep the road and a bridge over which it was necessary to pass. The major portion of the infantry were posted on a range of hills to the right of the road, and in some timber and ravines in their front. I was soon satisfied the fight for Raymond was to take place at this point. Orders were immediately sent back to move all our trains out of the road, for the remainder of Logan's division to advance as rapidly as possible, followed by Crocker's, which was to form the reserve.

. . . The battle opened with great fury on the center and the left center. . . . The enemy was handsomely repulsed and in full retreat. . . .

Pursuit was immediately commenced, and the town of Raymond was entered by our troops at 5 p.m., the enemy having passed through without stopping, toward Jackson, via Mississippi Springs. In this short but spirited engagement our loss in killed was 69. . . . Our loss in wounded was 341; missing 30. The enemy's loss was, in killed, 103; wounded and prisoners, 720; two pieces of cannon disabled, besides a quantity of small arms.[30]

Although the fighting lasted several hours, Gregg's Brigade never had a chance against McPherson's two divisions, and the Confederates retreated through the town, passing up dinner being served by the local ladies. The advancing Union soldiers quickly took advantage of the ladies' hospitality!

While a comparatively insignificant action, Grant realized that there must be more Confederates in Jackson, and so he decided to advance to that city and capture it before turning back west. This he subsequently did.

Report of Maj. Gen. Ulysses S. Grant, USA, Commanding Army of the Tennessee

On the night of May 12, after orders had been given for the corps of McClernand and Sherman to march to the railroad by parallel roads, the former in the direction of Edwards Station and the latter to a point on the railroad between Edwards Station and Bolton, the order was changed, and both were directed to move toward Raymond. This was in consequence of the enemy having retreated toward Jackson, after his defeat at Raymond, and of information that re-inforcements were daily arriving at Jackson, and that General Joe Johnston was hourly expected there to take command in person. I therefore determined to make sure of that place and leave no enemy in my rear.[31]

Narrative of Maj. Gen. Ulysses S. Grant, USA, Commanding Army of the Tennessee

Personal Memoirs

When the news reached me of McPherson's victory at Raymond about sundown my position was with Sherman. I decided at once to turn the whole column towards Jackson and capture that place without delay.

Pemberton was now on my left, with, as I supposed, about 18,000 men; in fact, as I learned afterwards, with nearly 50,000. A force was also collecting on my right, at Jackson, the point where all the railroads communicating with Vicksburg connect. All the enemy's supplies of men and stores would come by that point. As I hoped in the end to besiege Vicksburg I must first destroy all possibility of aid. I therefore determined to move swiftly towards Jackson, destroy or drive any force in that direction and then turn upon Pemberton. But by moving against Jackson, I uncovered my own communication. So I finally decided to have none—to cut loose altogether from my base and move my whole force eastward. I then had no fears for my communications, and if I moved quickly enough could turn upon Pemberton before he could attack me in the rear.

Accordingly, all previous orders given during the day for the movements on the 13th were annulled by new ones. McPherson was ordered at daylight to move on Clinton, ten miles from Jackson; Sherman was notified of my determination to capture Jackson and work from there westward. He was ordered to start at four in the morning and march to Raymond. McClernand was ordered to march with three divisions by Dillion's to Raymond. One was left to guard the crossing of the Big Black.[32]

On May 13, McPherson's and Sherman's corps both fought briefly in heavy rain and forced the Confederate defenders of Jackson to evacuate the capital. The Federals proceeded to destroy everything of military value, especially focusing on the railroads. General Johnston and his small command retreated to the north.

This critical decision to change plans and not only sever Vicksburg's principal supply line but also destroy its primary supply base (as well as that for other parts of the Confederacy) was a significant threat to the rebels. Often overlooked, but of great importance, was the fact that Pemberton's communication with Richmond, and particularly with President Davis, was eliminated. Pemberton would now have to operate without any further advice or orders from Jefferson Davis. This did not make it any easier for the officer to properly command.

Stop 5 is the Old Capitol Building in Jackson, and it is somewhat representative of the importance of that city to supplying Vicksburg. The structure is one of the city's few remnants from the Civil War. The entire area has urbanized, so the route to the Old Capitol is simply the easier way, not reminiscent of the war years. The building stands about 20.0 miles east of the Raymond Battlefield. Depart the battlefield eastbound on MS 18. Continue on MS 18 about 10.0 miles to the intersection with I-20. Merge onto I-20, and travel east toward Meridian. Drive almost 6.0 miles, and take Exit 46 toward Grenada/Memphis on I-55. Proceed north about 1.4 miles, and take Exit 96A toward the Convention Complex on East Pearl Street. At the intersection with State Street, turn right (north) onto South State Street, and you will almost immediately see the Old Capitol on the right (east). Park where convenient. Visit www.mdah.ms.gov to find days and hours for visitation.

Stop 5—*The Old Capitol Building*

Critical Decisions: (11) Grant Bypasses Vicksburg and Severs the Confederate Supply Line, (12) Grant Limits His Dependence on His Supply Line, (13) Grant Strikes at Jackson, (14) Johnston Determines He Cannot Assist Pemberton

Grant Bypasses Vicksburg and Severs the Confederate Supply Line

Grant's original decision to bypass Vicksburg in order to sever the Southern Railroad of Mississippi continued to apply here in Jackson. Until now, he had not actually cut the railroad. However, that would change on the thirteenth, when McPherson's corps would do so on the way to capturing Jackson. As noted above, severing communication with the rest of the Confederacy was of almost equal importance to seizing the city. This consideration undoubtedly affected Pemberton's decision-making.

Report of Maj. Gen. Ulysses S. Grant, USA, Commanding Army of the Tennessee

McPherson moved on the 13th to Clinton, destroyed the railroad and telegraph, and captured some important dispatches from General Pemberton to General Gregg, who had commanded the day before in the Battle of Raymond. Sherman moved to a parallel position on the Mississippi Springs and Jackson road. McClernand moved to a point near Raymond.[33]

However, Grant was no longer content merely to sever Vicksburg's main supply line. He would attempt to destroy the entire Confederate supply depot at Jackson.

Grant Limits His Dependence on His Supply Line

Up until his arrival in Jackson, Grant had depended to a limited extent on his supply line to provide essential supplies, particularly ammunition, while he maneuvered east of Vicksburg. However, after successfully capturing Jackson, the general ordered his men to take advantage of available supplies there in preparation for marching west to their target city. Leaving the capital, Grant would temporarily operate without any supply line.

Narrative of Maj. Gen. Ulysses S. Grant, USA, Commanding Army of the Tennessee

Personal Memoirs

But by moving against Jackson, I uncovered my own communication. So I finally decided to have none—to cut loose altogether from my base and move my whole force eastward. I then had no fears for my communications, and if I moved quickly enough could turn upon Pemberton before he could attack me in the rear.[34]

This bold decision by the Union commander was indicative of his style of command: he would do anything to get the job done.

Johnston Determines He Cannot Assist Pemberton

With the situation deteriorating around Vicksburg, President Davis finally ordered Gen. Joseph E. Johnston, nominally the theater commander, to proceed to Jackson and personally supervise Pemberton while providing all possible aid.

Message to Gen. Joseph E. Johnston, CSA, Commanding Relief Force

War Department, Richmond, Va., May 9, 1863
General Joseph E. Johnston, Tullahoma, Tenn,:

> Proceed at once to Mississippi and take chief command of the forces there, giving to those in the field, as far as practicable, the encouragement and benefit of your personal direction. Arrange to take with you for temporary service, or to be followed without delay, 3,000 good troops, who will be substituted in General Bragg's army by a large number of prisoners recently returned from the Arkansas Post capture, and reorganized, now on their way to General Pemberton. Stop them at the point most convenient to join General Bragg. You will find re-inforcements from General Beauregard to General Pemberton, and more may be expected. Acknowledge receipt.
>
> J. A. Seddon
> Secretary of War[35]

Although still in ill health, Johnston immediately headed to Jackson. Upon arrival there, he surveyed the situation.

Report of Gen. Joseph E. Johnston, CSA, Commanding Relief Force

Jackson, Miss., May 13, 1863
James A. Seddon:
> I arrived this evening, finding the enemy's force between this place and General Pemberton, cutting off the communication. I am too late.
>
> J. E. Johnston
> General[36]

This statement indicates that the general did not believe he could be of any help to Pemberton. The fact that Pemberton tended to not comply with Johnston's orders in order to protect Vicksburg did not help. Johnston would continue to be upset with Pemberton's failure to obey his orders, as incomprehensible as they appeared to the Vicksburg commander.

However, Johnston was correct in adhering to the military concept that it was better to give up a military objective such as the Hill City, but keep the defending army intact to fight another day. The alternative was fall back into the objective, suffer a siege, and surrender both the objective and the defending army. Yet Johnston simply went through the motions of attempting to unite with Pemberton and his army. Historians tend to believe that these movements were insincere, as Johnston perceived no chance for Pemberton to stop Grant before Vicksburg, and the loss of both city and army if Pemberton retreated there. The following reports are typical.

Reports of Gen. Joseph E. Johnston, CSA, Commanding Relief Force

Camp, Between Livingston and Brownsville, via Jackson and Montgomery, May 18, [1863]
General S. Cooper:

Lieutenant-General Pemberton was attacked on the morning of the 16th near Edwards Depot, and after nine hours' fighting was compelled to fall back behind Big Black. Mr. Shelton, of this neighborhood, wrote last night that he was just from Lieutenant-General Pemberton's headquarters, and that the army was falling back to Vicksburg. Mr. Robinson, just from Bovina last night, made the same report. There are two months' provisions in Vicksburg. It must ultimately fall unless we can assemble an army to relieve. I can gather in a few days 11,000, besides a garrison at Port Hudson. Send us [R. H.] Anderson's cavalry regiment from the Isle of Hope Ga. We need it greatly.

J. E. Johnston
General[37]

Jackson, Miss, May 27, 1863
Hon. James A. Seddon, Secretary of War, Richmond, VA

On the 20th and 21st instant, the brigades of Generals Gist, Ector, and McNair joined my command. The last troops of Brigadier-General Evans' arrived on the day before yesterday. Major-General Loring, with his command, arrived here about the 19th instant, and Brigadier-General Maxey's brigade on the 23rd instant.

The troops above mentioned, with General Breckinridge's division, of General Bragg's army, will make a force of about 23,000 effective men. Grant's army is estimated at 60,000 or 80,000 men, and his troops are worth double the number of Northeastern troops. We cannot relieve General Pemberton except by defeating Grant, who is believed to be fortifying. We must make the attempt with such a force as the government can furnish for the object; unless more may be expected, the attempt must be made with the force now here and that coming. If possible, however, additional troops should be sent to make up an army of at least 30,000 men—infantry. Even that force will be small for the object. An army of 23,000 men for offensive operations against Grant seems to me too small, considering his large force. We need very much good general officers.[38]

J. E. Johnston
General

Sadly for the Confederacy, Johnston would never display the commanding effort to assist Pemberton before he retreated into Vicksburg. Likewise, he would never come to assist Pemberton in escaping from the Hill City. This decision-making eventually sealed the fate of Vicksburg.

Stop 6 is the Champion Hill Battlefield, which is about 24.0 miles west of the Old Capitol Building. Again, because of the urban buildup, we will take the non-historic interstate most of the way to this site. When able, turn south onto State Street, and continue south on it about 2.0 miles, following the signs to merge onto I-20 heading west toward Vicksburg. Continue west about 17.0 miles to Exit 27 toward Bolton. Merge northwest onto the Bolton Brownsville Road, but continue only about 250 feet. Then turn left (west) onto the Askew Ferry Road, which parallels the interstate going west. Follow the Askew Ferry Road 3.3 miles until the intersection with South Farr Road. Follow South Farr Road about 1.3 miles to the intersection with Champion Hill Road. Turn right (west) onto Champion Hill Road, and continue 1.7 miles to the junction with Billy Fields Road on the left. Turn left (southeast) onto Billy Fields Road, and continue 1.4 miles to the intersection with D. J. Johnson Road. This is the location of the "crossroads" in the literature about the battle. Park safely, and get out and view the historical markers and terrain.

Stop 6—Champion Hill Battlefield

Critical Decisions: (12) Grant Limits His Dependence on His Supply Line, (15) Pemberton Mismanages His Defense of Vicksburg

The Battle of Champion Hill essentially set the stage for Vicksburg's fate. The ultimate Union victory sent the Confederates scrambling; the troops made a disastrous retreat west to the Big Black River railroad bridge crossing it.

Grant Limits His Dependence on His Supply Line

Having successfully destroyed most everything of military value in Jackson, Grant ordered a westward advance, partially along the Southern Railroad of Mississippi, toward his ultimate goal of Vicksburg. Logistically, he was totally out of position to obtain supplies via a Union supply line; his enemy stood between him and his supply base on the Mississippi River. Yet this did not hinder Grant. His men continued to live off the land as they maneuvered east of Vicksburg.

One factor that could severely damage the Union commander's plan was his unprotected rear, which was vulnerable to attack by Johnston's Command. Although this was an opportunity for the relief army commander to exploit, Johnston had, in fact, retreated north all the way to Canton! He had positioned himself squarely out of the range of providing immediate assistance to Pemberton and the Confederacy. Yet Johnston sent Pemberton orders to attack Grant's rear.

Report of Gen. Joseph E. Johnston, CSA, Commanding Army of Relief

Jackson, May 13, 1863—8:40 p.m.
Lieutenant-General Pemberton:

I have lately arrived, and learn that Major-General Sherman is between us, with four divisions, at Clinton. It is important to re-establish communications, that you may be re-inforced. If practicable, come upon his rear at once. To beat such a detachment, would be of immense value. The troops here could co-operate. All the strength you can quickly assemble should be brought. Time is all-important.

Your obedient servant, J. E. Johnston[39]

Grant received a copy of Johnston's above message from a "loyal man." He responded.

Narrative of Maj. Gen. Ulysses S. Grant, USA, Commanding Army of the Tennessee

Personal Memoirs

Receiving this [above] dispatch on the 14th I ordered McPherson to move promptly in the morning back to Bolton, the nearest point where Johnston could reach the road. Bolton is about twenty miles west of Jackson. I also informed McClernand of the capture of Jackson and sent him the following order: "It is evidently the design of the enemy to get north of us and cross the Big Black, and beat us into Vicksburg. We must not allow them to do this. Turn all your forces towards Bolton station, and make all dispatch in getting there. Move troops by the most direct road from wherever they may be on the receipt of this order."[40]

Grant began to face his army west. Still unhindered, on the sixteenth he advanced west past Bolton along three lines of approach, wary of possible interdiction by his enemy. His caution paid off as his three corps approached the area of Champion Hill. Grant's short report of the battle follows.

Report of Maj. Gen. Ulysses S. Grant, USA, Commanding Army of the Tennessee

Passing to the front, I found Hovey's division, of the Thirteenth Army Corps, at a halt with our skirmishers and the enemy's pickets near each other. Hovey was bringing his troops into line ready for battle, and could have brought on an engagement at any moment. The enemy had taken up a very strong position on a narrow ridge, his left resting on a height where the road makes a sharp turn to the left, approaching Vicksburg. The top of the ridge and the precipitous hillside to the left of the road are covered by a dense forest and undergrowth. To the right of the road the timber extends a short distance down the hill, and then opens into cultivated fields on a gentle slope and into a valley, extending for a considerable distance. On the road and into a wooded ravine and hillside Hovey's division was disposed for the attack. McPherson's two divisions—all of his corps with him on the march from Millikin's Bend, until Ransom's brigade arrived the day after the battle—were thrown to the right of the road (properly speaking, the enemy's rear), but I would not permit an attack to be commenced until I could hear from McClernand, who was advancing with four divisions, two of them on a road intersecting the Jackson road about 1 mile from where the troops above were placed, and about the center of the enemy's line;

the other two divisions on a road still north, and nearly the same distance off.

I soon heard from McClernand through members of his staff and my own, whom I had sent to him early in the morning, and found by the nearest practical route of communication he was 2 ½ miles distant. I sent several successive messages to him to push forward with all rapidity. There had been continuous firing between Hovey's skirmishers and the Confederate advance, which by 11 o'clock grew into a battle. For some time this division drew the brunt of the conflict; but finding the enemy too strong for them, at the insistence of Hovey, I directed first one and then a second brigade from Crocker's division to re-inforce him. All this time Logan's division was working upon the enemy's left and rear, and weakened his front attack most wonderfully. The troops here opposing us evidently far outnumbered ours. Expecting McClernand momentarily with four divisions, including Blair's, I never felt a doubt of the result. He did not arrive, however, until the enemy had been driven from the field, and after a terrible contest of hours, with a heavy loss of killed, wounded, and prisoners, and a number of pieces of artillery.

It was found afterward that the Vicksburg road, after following the ridge in a southerly direction for about 1 mile, and to where it intersected one of the Raymond roads, turns almost to the west, down the hill and across the valley in which Logan was operating on the rear of the enemy. One brigade of Logan's division had, unconscious of this important fact, penetrated nearly to this road, and compelled the enemy to retreat to prevent capture. As it was, much of his artillery and Loring's division of his army were cut off, besides the prisoners captured.[41]

Pemberton Mismanages His Defense of Vicksburg

In hindsight, Lieut. Gen. John C. Pemberton generally did not understand his opponent's movements and distractions until it was too late to confront them. The various cavalry raids demonstrated the Confederates' confusion over who was trying to do what.

Pemberton's mismanagement could be discussed at every stop on this driving tour of the critical decisions of the Vicksburg Campaign. For clarity, I have not addressed this concern until this stop and the next one. Unfortunately for the rebels, the Confederate commander did not confront the entire advancing Union army with his own command until the Battle of Champion Hill. Certainly, Pemberton's and Johnston's failure to unite and confront the Federal army resulted in the ultimate loss of the bastion on the river. For example, this exchange of messages demonstrates Pemberton's concern for defending Vicksburg over anything else.

Message from Lieut. Gen. John C. Pemberton to Pres. Jefferson Davis

Vicksburg, May 12, 1863

Jefferson Davis, Richmond, Va., and
General Johnston, Tullahoma:

The enemy is apparently moving in heavy force towards Edwards Depot, Southern Railroad. With my limited force, I will do all I can to meet him. That will be the field of battle if I can carry forward sufficient force, leaving troops enough to secure the safety of this place. Re-inforcements are arriving very slowly; only 1,500 have come as yet. I urgently ask that more be sent; also 3,000 cavalry to be at once sent to operate on this line. I urge this as a positive necessity. The enemy largely outnumbers me, and I am obliged to hold back large forces at the ferries on Big Black, lest he cross and take this place. I am also compelled to keep a considerable force on either flank of Vicksburg, out of supporting distance of Edwards, to prevent his approach in those directions.

J. C. Pemberton[42]

The below message is in response to Johnston's aforementioned communication dated May 13.

Message from Lieut. Gen. John C. Pemberton to Gen. Joseph E. Johnston

Bovina, May 14, 1863

I have the honor to acknowledge receipt of your communication. I move at once with whole available force (about 16,000) [actually more like 23,000] from Edwards Depot, leaving Vaughn's brigade, about 1,500 at Big Black Bridge. Tilghman's brigade, 1,500, now at Baldwin's Ferry, I have ordered to bring up the rear of my column; he will be, however, from 15 to 20 miles behind it. Baldwin's Ferry will be left necessarily unprotected. To hold Vicksburg are Smith's and Forney's divisions, extending from Snyder's Mill to Warrenton, numbering 7,500 effective men. The men have been marching several days, are much fatigued, and I fear will straggle much. In directing this move, I do not think you fully comprehend the position that Vicksburg will be left in, but I comply at once with your order.[43]

Message from Gen. Joseph E. Johnston to Lieut. Gen. John C. Pemberton

Canton Road, Ten Miles from Jackson, May 15, 1863—8:30 a.m.
Lieutenant-General Pemberton, Commanding, etc.:

Your dispatch of yesterday just received. Our being compelled to leave Jackson makes your plan impracticable. The only mode by which we can unite is by your moving directly to Clinton, informing me, that we may move to that point with about 6,000. I have no means of estimating the enemy's force at Jackson. The principal officers here differ very widely. I fear he will fortify if time is left him. Let me hear from you immediately. General Maxey was ordered back to Brookhaven. You probably have time to make him join you. Do so before he has time to move away.

Most respectfully,
J. E. Johnston[44]

Pemberton responded by changing his plans again.

Message from Lieut. Gen. John C. Pemberton to Gen. Joseph E. Johnston

Four Miles South of Edwards Depot, May 16, 1863
General Joseph E. Johnston:

Your letter, written on the road to Canton, was received this morning at 6:30. It found this army on the middle road to Raymond. The order of countermarch has been issued.

J. C. Pemberton[45]

Pemberton again changed plans, setting up the confrontation with the Union army. Pemberton described the Battle of Champion Hill in the following report. Although lengthy, it shows his frustration and inability to command.

Report of Lieut. Gen. John C. Pemberton, CSA, Commanding Army of Vicksburg

I immediately directed a countermarch, or rather a retrograde movement, by reversing the column as it then stood, for the purpose of returning to Edwards Depot to take the Brownsville road, and thence to proceed toward Clinton by a route north of the railroad. A written reply to General Johnston's instructions, in which I notified him that the countermarch had been ordered and of the route I should take, was dispatched in haste, and without allowing myself sufficient time to take a copy.

Just as this reverse movement commenced, the enemy drove in Colonel Adams' cavalry pickets, and opened with artillery at long range on the head of my column on the Raymond road. Not knowing whether this was an attack in force or simply an armed reconnaissance, and being anxious to obey the instructions of General Johnston, I directed the continuance of the movement, giving the necessary instructions for securing the safety of the wagon train. The demonstrations of the enemy soon becoming more serious, orders were sent to division commanders to form in line of battle on the cross-road from the Clinton to the Raymond Road, Loring on the right, Bowen in the center, and Stevenson on the left. Major-General Stevenson was instructed to make the necessary dispositions for the protection of the trains then on the Clinton road and crossing Baker's Creek. The line of battle was quickly formed, without any interference on the part of the enemy. The position selected was naturally a strong one, and all approaches from the front well covered. A short time after the formation of the line, Loring's division was thrown back so as to cover the military road, it being reported that the enemy had appeared in that direction. The enemy made his first demonstration on our right, but after a lively artillery duel for an hour or more, this attack was relinquished, and a large force was thrown against our left, where skirmishing became heavy about 10 o'clock, and the battle began in earnest along Stevenson's entire front about noon.

Just at this time a column of the enemy were seen moving in front of our center toward the right. [John C.] Landis' battery, of Bowen's division, opened upon and soon broke this column, and compelled it to retire. I then directed Major-General Loring to move forward and crush the enemy in his front, and directed General Bowen to co-operate with him in the movement. Immediately on the receipt of my message, General Bowen rode up and announced his readiness to execute his part of the movement as soon as Major-General Loring should advance. No movement was made by Major-General Loring, he informing me that the enemy was too strongly posted to be attacked, but he would seize the first opportunity to assault, if one should offer. The enemy still making strenuous efforts to turn Major-General Stevenson's left flank, compelled him to make a similar movement toward the left, thus extending his own line and making a gap between his and Bowen's divisions. General Bowen was ordered to keep this interval closed, and the same instructions were sent to General Loring in reference to the interval between his and General Bowen's division.

General Stevenson having informed me that unless re-inforced he would be unable to resist the heavy and repeated attacks along his whole line, Bowen was ordered to send one brigade to his assistance, which was promptly brought forward under Col. F. M. Cockrell, and in a very short period of time his remaining brigade, under the command of Brig. Gen. Martin E. Green, was put in, and the two together, under their gallant leaders, charged the enemy, and for the time turned the tide of battle in our favor, again displaying the heroic courage which this veteran division has made conspicuous on so many stricken fields.

The enemy still continued to move troops from his left to his right, thus increasing his vastly superior forces against Stevenson's and Bowen's divisions. Feeling assured that there was no important force in his front, I dispatched several staff officers in rapid succession to Major-General Loring, ordering him to move all but one brigade (Tilghman's, which was directed to hold the Raymond road and cover the bridge and ford at Baker's Creek) to the left as rapidly as possible. To the first of these messages, sent about 2 p.m., answer was returned by Major-General Loring that the enemy was in strong force in his front, and endeavoring to flank him. Hearing no firing on the right, I repeated my orders to Major-General Loring, explaining the condition of affairs on the left, and directed him to put his two left brigades into the fight as soon as possible. In the transmission of these various messages to and fro, over a distance of more than a mile, much valuable time was necessarily consumed, which the enemy did not fail to take advantage of.

About 4 p.m. a part of Stevenson's division broke badly and fell back in great disorder, but was partially rallied by the strenuous exertions of myself and staff, and put back under their own offi-cers into the fight, but observing that large numbers of men were abandoning the field on Stevenson's left, deserting their comrades, who in this moment of greatest trial stood manfully at their posts, I rode up to General Stevenson, and informing him that I had re-peatedly ordered two brigades of General Loring's division to his assistance, and that I was momentarily expecting them, asked him whether he could hold his position; he replied that he could not; that he was fighting from 60,000 to 80,000 men. I then told him I would endeavor myself to find General Loring and hasten him up, and started immediately with that object. I presently met Brigadier-General Buford's brigade, of Loring's division, on the march and in rear of the right of Bowen's division.

Colonel Cockrell, commanding the First Missouri Brigade, having in person some time previously urgently asked for re-inforce-ments, which (none of Loring's troops having come up) I was unable to give him, one regiment of Buford's brigade was detached at once and directed to his support; the remainder of Buford's brigade was moved as rapidly as possible to the assistance of General Stevenson.

Finding that the enemy's vastly superior numbers were pressing all my forces engaged steadily back into old fields, where all advan-tages of position would be in his favor, I felt it was too late to save the day, even should Brigadier-General Featherstone's brigade, of Loring's division, come up immediately. I could, however, learn noth-ing of General Loring's whereabouts; several of my staff were in search of him, but it was not until after General Bowen had personally in-formed me that he could not hold his position longer, and not until af-ter I had ordered the retreat, that General Loring, with Featherstone's brigade, moving, as I subsequently learned, by a country road which was considerably longer than the direct route, reached the position on the left known as Champion's Hill, where he was forming the line of battle when he received my order to cover the retreat.[46]

Loring's failure to promptly obey orders hindered the Confederates' ability to counter the Union advance, but would not have ultimately changed the outcome of the battle.

Stop 7 is about 10.0 miles west of the Champion Hill Battlefield, at the Big Black River. Turn around, and drive west-northwest on Billy Fields Road back to the intersection with Champion Hill Road. Turn left (west) on Champion Hill Road, crossing Baker's Creek in 0.4 mile, and continue about a mile to the intersection with Buck Reed Road. Turn right (north) onto Buck Reed Road, and cross the railroad tracks (old bed of the Southern Railroad of Mississippi). Immediately turn left (west) onto Cemetery Road (the old Jackson Road), and proceed about 1.7 miles to the junction with Old Highway 80 in Edwards. Follow it through town by a left onto Magnolia Street and then a right onto Vicksburg Avenue. Continue west on Old Highway 80 about 5.0 miles, and cross the Big Black River and then Clear Creek. Just beyond Clear Creek, turn left (south) onto Warriors Trail, continue south 0.2 mile to the Big Black River, and park. While leaving your vehicle, notice the old bridge piers just south of the present bridge piers.

Stop 7—Battle of the Big Black River Bridge

Critical Decision: (15) Pemberton Mismanages His Defense of Vicksburg

Pemberton Mismanages His Defense of Vicksburg

After the defeat at Champion Hill, Pemberton ordered a retreat west to the Big Black River, near where the Southern Railroad of Mississippi crossed that stream. His plan required that his remaining troops hold the position there to facilitate the regrouping of his army while waiting for W. W. Loring's division to rejoin his command. Unfortunately, this position was quickly overrun by the Union army.

Message from Lieut. Gen. John C. Pemberton to Gen. Joseph E. Johnston

Hdqrs. Dept. of Mississippi and Eastern Louisiana,
Vicksburg, Miss., May 17, 1863
General Joseph E. Johnston, Commanding, etc.:

General: Whilst writing my communication this morning, the enemy attacked me on my right, left, and center. My troops, although strongly posted behind breastworks and protected in rifle-pits, were forced from their positions, owing to the demoralization consequent upon the retreat of yesterday. Every effort is now being made to reorganize the troops, and it is hoped that their numbers, although greatly diminished by incidents narrated, will be speedily increased.

The army has fallen back to the line of intrenchments around Vicksburg. As stated in my communication of this morning, this retreat will render it necessary to abandon the works at Snyder's Mill, which has accordingly been ordered. All the ammunition possible will be saved. The heavy guns, however, will necessarily be abandoned.

Two companies will be left at that point for the purpose of making a demonstration, and of spiking the guns and destroying the remaining stores whenever the emergency may arise.

The works at Fort Pemberton, which may prove essential to a line along the Yalabusha [*sic*], have not been abandoned. The garrison of 200 men remain there.

I regret to say that as yet I have received no reliable information with regard to General Loring's division. It is reported, but I cannot trace the rumor to a reliable source, that he is crossing the Big Black River at some point below the Big Black Bridge.

In addition to the artillery lost yesterday, I regret to state that most of the artillery of Bowen's division is lost. Yesterday it was all successfully brought off, but to-day was abandoned in the trenches, almost without an effort to save it.

I greatly regret that I felt compelled to make the advance beyond the Big Black, which has proven so disastrous in its results.

J. C. Pemberton[47]

To Joseph E. Johnston's credit, he succinctly understood Pemberton's options and pointed them out to the Vicksburg commander.

Report of Gen. Joseph E. Johnston, CSA, Commanding Army of Relief

I immediately replied, May 17 [to Pemberton]:

If Hayne's Bluff be untenable, Vicksburg is of no value and cannot be held. If, therefore, you are invested in Vicksburg, you must ultimately surrender. Under such circumstances, instead of losing both troops and place, you must, if possible, save the troops. If it not too late, evacuate Vicksburg and its dependences, and march to the northeast.[48]

However, in fairness to John Pemberton, he visualized a different scenario in which it was better to attempt to retain the Hill City and its defenses.

Reports of Lieut. Gen. John C. Pemberton, CSA, Commanding Army of Vicksburg

The evacuation of Vicksburg! It meant the loss of the valuable stores and munitions of war collected for its defense; the fall of Port Hudson; the surrender of the Mississippi River, and the severance of the Confederacy. These were mighty interests, which, had I deemed the evacuation practicable in the sense which I interpreted General Johnston's instructions, might well have made me hesitate to execute them. I believed it to be in my power to hold Vicksburg. I knew and appreciated the earnest desire of the Government and of the people that it should be held. I knew, perhaps better than any other individual, under all the circumstances, its capacity for defense. As long ago as February 17 last, in a letter addressed to His Excellency the President, I had suggested the possibility of investment of Vicksburg by land and water, and for that reason the necessity of ample supplies of ammunition as well as of subsistence to stand a siege. My application met his favorable consideration, and additional ammunition was ordered. With proper economy of subsistence and ordnance stores, I knew that I could stand a siege. I had a firm reliance on the desire of the President and of General Johnston to do all that could be done to raise a siege. I felt that every effort would be made, and I believed it would be successful. With these convictions on my own mind, I immediately summoned a council of war composed of all my general officers. I laid before them General Johnston's communication, but desired them to confine the expression of their opinions to the question of practicability. Having obtained their views, the following communication was addressed to General Johnston:

Hdqrs. Department of Mississippi and Eastern Louisiana
Vicksburg, May 18, 1863

General Joseph E. Johnston: I have the honor to acknowledge the receipt of your communication, in reply to mine by the hands of Captain [Thomas] Henderson. In a subsequent letter of same date as this letter, I informed you that the men had failed to hold the trenches at Big Black Bridge, and that, as a consequence, Snyder's Mill was directed to be abandoned. On the receipt of your communication, I immediately assembled a council of war of the general officers of this command, and having laid your instructions before them, asked the free expression of their opinions as to the practicability of carrying them out. The opinion was unanimously expressed that it was impossible to withdraw the army from this position with such *morale* and material as to be of further service to the Confederacy. While the council of war was assembled, the guns of the enemy opened on the works, and it was at the same time reported that they were crossing the Yazoo River at Brandon's Ferry above Snyder's Mill. I have decided to hold Vicksburg as long as possible, with the firm hope that the Government may yet be able to assist me in keeping this obstruction to the enemy's free navigation of the Mississippi River. I still conceive it to be the most important point in the Confederacy.

Very respectfully, your obedient servant,

J. C. Pemberton
Lieutenant-General, Commanding.[49]

Unfortunately, while Pemberton firmly believed that he had taken the correct action in retreating into the Vicksburg defenses, Johnston remained accurate in his prediction of loss of both army and location. Pemberton failed to choose the lesser of two evils when he retreated into the defenses, ultimately surrendering his army and forfeiting the location—truly a significant failure for the Confederacy. This critical decision can certainly be considered a major turning point in the Civil War.

Stop 8 returns to the Vicksburg lines in Vicksburg National Military Park. Continue 1.8 miles west to the junction with Bovina Drive on the left. Turn right (north), and proceed 0.3 mile to the junction with Bovina Drive on your right. Continue 5.4 miles on Warriors Trail to the intersection with MS 27. Turn right (north) onto MS 27, and continue about 2.0 miles to the intersection with Old US 80. Turn left (west) onto Old US 80, which becomes Clay Street, and continue about 1.5 miles to the entrance to Vicksburg National Military Park. Park safely.

Stop 8—Back to the Vicksburg Lines

Critical Decisions: (16) Grant Assaults the Vicksburg Fortifications, (17) Grant Paroles the Confederate Prisoners

Grant Assaults the Vicksburg Fortifications

After Pemberton ordered his army to retreat into the Confederate fortifications surrounding Vicksburg, Grant immediately surrounded the embedded Confederate command. He knew he must decide whether to assault the enemy works or establish a siege. Grant's personal fear was having to remain in place, waiting for the Confederates to surrender. He believed that the Rebels were demoralized at present because of their recent defeats, and that they had not fully secured their works.

Message from Maj. Gen. Ulysses S. Grant to Rear Adm. David D. Porter

Rear of Vicksburg, Miss., May 19, 1863
Rear-Admiral David D. Porter,
Commanding Mississippi Squadron:

My forces are now investing Vicksburg. Sherman's forces run from the Mississippi River, above the city, 2 miles east. McPherson is to his left, and McClernand to the left of McPherson. If you can run down and throw shell in just back of the city, it would aid us, and demoralize an already badly beaten enemy. The enemy has not been able to return to the city with one-half of his forces.

We beat them badly on the 16th, near Edwards Station, and on the 17th, at Black River Bridge, taking about 6,000 prisoners, besides a large number killed and wounded.

Two divisions were also cut off from their retreat. And have gone eastward, many of their men throwing down their arms and leaving. The enemy only succeeded in getting back three pieces of artillery. I have instructed my quartermaster and commissary to send boats up to Lake's Landing with forage and provisions; will you please send a convoy? Please send a boat up to Hayne's Bluff, which I think is evacuated. Our cavalry have gone up to see.

U. S. Grant[50]

Rather than lose time conducting a siege, the Union commander made the critical decision to immediately assault the fortification protecting the Hill City and its river cannon. Wasting no time, he issued orders for an assault on May 19.

Orders of Maj. Gen. Ulysses S. Grant, USA, Commanding Army of the Tennessee

Special Orders   Headquarters, Department of the Tennessee
No. 134 Near Vicksburg, Miss., May 19, 1863—11:16 a.m.
Army corps commanders will push forward carefully, and gain as close position as possible to the enemy's works until 2:00 p.m. At that hour they will fire three volleys of artillery from all the pieces in position. This will be the signal for a general charge of all the corps along the whole line. When the works are carried, guards will be placed by all division commanders, to prevent their men from straggling from their companies.
     By order of Maj. Gen. U. S. Grant
     JNO A. RAWLINS
     Assistant Adjutant-General[51]

Unfortunately for the Union army, the assaults on the nineteenth failed. Reasoning that his troops had little time to position themselves, Grant ordered another, hopefully more coordinated, strike on May 22. While the Union achieved very limited success, this assault also failed. The Confederates displayed much higher morale than expected. The result of the two assaults was that Grant was forced to conduct a siege. Although the outcome was all but inevitable, nonetheless a huge effort on both sides began.

Over the course of many days, either the Confederate defenders would exhaust their food or ammunition, or the Federals would gradually move their siege lines so close to their opponent that a final assault would be successful.

Grant Paroles the Confederate Prisoners

Grant wasted no time in securing his line of circumvallation. He called for additional reinforcements and tightened the line. Also, the Union commander established a line of contravallation, commanded by Sherman, to protect against a possible attack by Johnston's small relief army.

By the beginning of July, the Union army was within only a few yards of the Confederate line in many locations, and Grant ordered an assault for July 6. However, John Pemberton had realized that his army was low on food, and Joseph Johnston was not going to come to the rescue. With no other realistic options, and perhaps believing that better surrender terms might be offered because of the upcoming Fourth of July Federal holiday, Pemberton proposed that a commission be established to discuss potential terms of surrender with his opponent.

Report of Lieut. Gen. John C. Pemberton, CSA, Commanding Army of Vicksburg

Maj. Gen. U. S. Grant Headquarters
Commanding United States Forces: Vicksburg, Miss., July 3, 1863

General: I have the honor to propose to you an armistice for several hours, with a view to arranging terms for the capitulation of Vicksburg. To this end, if agreeable to you, I will appoint three commissioners to meet a like number, to be named by yourself, at such place and hour to-day as you may find convenient.

I make this proposition to save the further effusion of blood, which otherwise must be shed to a frightful extent, feeling myself fully able to maintain my position for a yet indefinite period.

This communication will be handed you under a flag of truce by Maj. Gen. John S. Bowen.

Very respectfully, your obedient servant,

J. C. PEMBERTON
Lieutenant-General Commanding[52]

In the course of two hours the annexed reply was received:

Headquarters Department of the Tennessee
In the Field near Vicksburg, Miss., July 3, 1863
Lieut. Gen. J. C. Pemberton
Commanding Confederate Forces, etc.:

General: Your note of this date is just received, proposing an armistice for several hours, for the purpose of arranging terms of capitulation through commissioners to be appointed, etc.

The useless effusion of blood you propose stopping by this course can be ended at any time you may choose, by an unconditional surrender of the city and garrison. Men who have shown so much endurance and courage as those now in Vicksburg will always challenge the respect of an adversary, and I can assure you will be treated with all the respect due to prisoners of war.

I do not favor the proposition of appointing commissioners to arrange terms of capitulation, because I have no terms other than those indicated above.

I am, general, very respectfully, your obedient servant,

U. S. Grant
Major-General.[53]

On the afternoon of May 3, Lieut. Gen. John Pemberton and Maj. Gen. John Bowen, who had known Grant before the war, met with the Union commander under a flag of truce. It was Bowen's plan to obtain a satisfactory surrender, and he neglected to inform his commander that he had used Pemberton's name to set up the meeting. While Grant and Pemberton talked of the old days, the details were generally agreed on. After some back-and-forth, Grant sent the below final message to Pemberton early on July 4, to which the Confederate immediately agreed.

Message from Maj. Gen. Ulysses S. Grant
to Lieut. Gen. John C. Pemberton

Headquarters Department of the Tennessee
Before Vicksburg, Miss., July 4, 1863
Lieut. Gen. J. C. Pemberton
Commanding Confederate Forces, Vicksburg, Miss:

General: I have the honor to acknowledge the receipt of your communication of 3rd July. The amendment proposed by you cannot be acceded to in full. It will be necessary to furnish every officer and man with a parole signed by himself, which, with the completion of the roll of prisoners, will necessarily take some time. Again, I can make no stipulations with regard to the treatment of citizens and their private property. While I do not propose to cause them any undue annoyance or loss, I cannot consent to leave myself under any restraint by stipulations. The property which officers will be allowed to take with them will be as stated in my proposition of last evening; that is, officers will be allowed their private baggage and side-arms, and mounted officers one horse each. If you mean by your proposition for each brigade to march to the front of the lines now occupied by it, and stack arms at 10 o'clock a.m., and then return to the inside and there remain as prisoners until properly paroled, I will make no objection to it. Should no notification be received of your acceptance of my terms by 9 o'clock a.m. I shall regard them as having been rejected, and shall act accordingly. Should these terms be accepted, white flags should be displayed along your lines to prevent such of my troops as may not have been notified, from firing upon your men.

I am, general, very respectfully, your obedient servant,

U. S. Grant
Major-General[54]

Grant obviously had taken time to analyze what to do with some thirty thousand prisoners upon the surrender of Vicksburg. He decided that paroling them was the best solution.

Narrative of Maj. Gen. Ulysses S. Grant, USA, Commanding Army of the Tennessee

Personal Memoirs

By the terms of the cartel [written agreement] then in force, prisoners captured by either army were required to be forwarded as soon as possible to either Aiken's landing below Dutch Gap on the James River, or to Vicksburg, there to be exchanged, or paroled until they could be exchanged. There was a Confederate commissioner at Vicksburg, authorized to make the exchange. I did not propose to take him a prisoner, but to leave him free to perform the functions of his office. Had I insisted upon an unconditional surrender there would have been over thirty thousand men to transport to Cairo, very much to the inconvenience of the army on the Mississippi. Thence the prisoners would have had to be transported by rail to Washington or Baltimore; thence again by steamer to Aiken's—all at very great expense. At Aiken's they would have had to be paroled, because the Confederates did not have Union prisoners to give in exchange. Then again Pemberton's army was largely composed of men whose homes were in the South-west; I knew many of them were tired of the war and would get home just as soon as they could. A large number of them had voluntarily come into our lines during the siege, and requested to be sent north where they could get employment until the war was over and they could go to their homes.[55]

This critical decision by U. S. Grant saved the United States government untold thousands of dollars and thousands of hours of labor in transferring these prisoners. While some of these men did indeed return to the Confederate armies illegally without being exchanged, their parole freed up the Army of the Tennessee to participate in other activities.

This concludes the driving tour of the critical decisions of the Vicksburg Campaign.

APPENDIX II

UNION ORDER OF BATTLE[1]

ARMY OF THE TENNESSEE
Maj. Gen. Ulysses S. Grant

ESCORT
4th Illinois Cavalry, Company A
ENGINEERS
1st Battalion, Bissell's Engineer Regiment of the West

HERRON'S DIVISION (reported directly to Grant—not assigned to a corps)
Maj. Gen. Francis J. Herron

FIRST BRIGADE
Brig. Gen. William Vandever
37th Illinois
26th Indiana
20th Iowa
34th Iowa
38th Iowa
1st Missouri Light Artillery, Battery E
1st Missouri Light Artillery, Battery F

SECOND BRIGADE
  Brig. Gen. William W. Orme
  94th Illinois
  19th Iowa
  20th Wisconsin
  1st Missouri Light Artillery, Battery B

NINTH CORPS
  Maj. Gen. John G. Parke

FIRST DIVISION
  Brig. Gen. Thomas Welsh

FIRST BRIGADE
  Col. Henry Bowman
  36th Massachusetts
  17th Michigan
  27th Michigan
  45th Pennsylvania

THIRD BRIGADE
  Col. Daniel Leasure
  2nd Michigan
  8th Michigan
  20th Michigan
  79th New York
  100th Pennsylvania

ARTILLERY
  1st Pennsylvania Light Artillery, Company D

SECOND DIVISION
  Brig. Gen. Robert B. Potter

FIRST BRIGADE
  Col. Simon G. Griffin
  6th New Hampshire
  9th New Hampshire
  7th Rhode Island

SECOND BRIGADE
  Brig. Gen. Edward Ferrero

35th Massachusetts
11th New Hampshire
51st New York
51st Pennsylvania

THIRD BRIGADE
Col. Benjamin C. Christ
29th Massachusetts
46th New York
50th Pennsylvania

ARTILLERY
2nd New York Light Artillery, Battery L

ARTILLERY RESERVE
2nd United States Artillery, Battery E

THIRTEENTH CORPS
Maj. Gen. John A. McClernand
Maj. Gen. Edward O. C. Ord

ESCORT
3rd Illinois Cavalry, Company L

PIONEERS
Patterson's Kentucky Company of Engineers and Mechanics

NINTH DIVISION (posted at the Big Black River Bridge)
Brig. Gen. Peter J. Osterhaus

FIRST BRIGADE
Col. James Keigwin
118th Illinois
49th Indiana
69th Indiana
7th Kentucky
120th Ohio

SECOND BRIGADE
Col. Daniel W. Lindsey
54th Indiana
22nd Kentucky
16th Ohio

42nd Ohio
114th Ohio

CAVALRY
2nd Illinois (5 companies)
3rd Illinois (3 companies)
6th Missouri (7 companies)

ARTILLERY
Capt. Jacob T. Foster
7th Battery Michigan Light Artillery
1st Battery Wisconsin Light Artillery

TENTH DIVISION
Brig. Gen. Andrew J. Smith

ESCORT
4th Indiana Cavalry, Company C

FIRST BRIGADE
Brig. Gen. Stephen G. Burbridge
16th Indiana
60th Indiana
67th Indiana
83rd Ohio
96th Ohio
23rd Wisconsin

SECOND BRIGADE
Col. William J. Landram
77th Illinois
97th Illinois
130th Illinois
19th Kentucky
48th Ohio

ARTILLERY
Chicago Mercantile Battery
17th Battery Ohio Light Artillery

TWELFTH DIVISION
Brig. Gen. Alvin P. Hovey

ESCORT
1st Indiana Cavalry, Company C

FIRST BRIGADE
Brig. Gen. George F. McGinnis
Brig. Gen. William T. Spicely
11th Indiana
24th Indiana
34th Indiana
46th Indiana
29th Wisconsin

SECOND BRIGADE
Col. James R. Slack
87th Illinois
47th Indiana
24th Iowa
28th Iowa

ARTILLERY
1st Missouri Light Artillery, Battery A
2nd Battery Ohio Light Artillery
16th Battery Ohio Light Artillery

FOURTEENTH DIVISION
Brig. Gen. Eugene A. Carr

ESCORT
3rd Illinois Cavalry, Company G

FIRST BRIGADE
Brig. Gen. William P. Benton
Col. Henry D. Washburne
Col. David Shunk
Brig. Gen. William P. Benton
33rd Illinois
99th Illinois
8th Indiana
18th Indiana

SECOND BRIGADE
Brig. Gen. Michael K. Lawler
21st Iowa

22nd Iowa
11th Wisconsin

ARTILLERY
2nd Illinois Light Artillery, Battery A
1st Battery Indiana Light Artillery

FIFTEENTH CORPS
Maj. Gen. William T. Sherman
Maj. Gen. Frederick Steele

FIRST DIVISION
Maj. Gen. Frederick Steele
Brig. Gen. John M. Thayer

FIRST BRIGADE
Col. Francis H. Manter
Col. Bernard G. Farrar
13th Illinois
27th Missouri
29th Missouri
30th Missouri
31st Missouri
32nd Missouri

SECOND BRIGADE
Col. Charles R. Woods
25th Iowa
31st Iowa
3rd Missouri
12th Missouri
17th Missouri
76th Ohio

THIRD BRIGADE
Brig. Gen. John M. Thayer
4th Iowa
9th Iowa
26th Iowa
30th Iowa

ARTILLERY
1st Battery Iowa Light Artillery

2nd Missouri Light Artillery, Battery F
4th Battery Ohio Light Artillery

CAVALRY

15th Illinois, Company H (Kane County Independent Cavalry)
3rd Illinois, Company D

SECOND DIVISION
Maj. Gen. Frank P. Blair Jr.

FIRST BRIGADE
Col. Giles A. Smith
113th Illinois
116th Illinois
6th Missouri
8th Missouri
13th United States, 1st Battalion

SECOND BRIGADE
Col. Thomas K. Smith
Brig. Gen. Joseph A. J. Lightburn
55th Illinois
127th Illinois
83rd Indiana
54th Ohio
57th Ohio

THIRD BRIGADE
Brig. Gen. Hugh Ewing
30th Ohio
37th Ohio
47th Ohio
4th West Virginia

ARTILLERY
1st Illinois Light Artillery, Battery A
1st Illinois Light Artillery, Battery B
1st Illinois Light Artillery, Battery H
8th Battery Ohio Light Artillery

CAVALRY
Thielemann's (Illinois) Battalion, Companies A and B
10th Missouri, Company C

THIRD DIVISION
Brig. Gen. James M. Tuttle

FIRST BRIGADE
Brig. Gen. Ralph P. Buckland
Col. William L. McMillen
114th Illinois
93rd Indiana
72nd Ohio
95th Ohio

SECOND BRIGADE
Brig. Gen. Joseph A. Mower
47th Illinois
5th Minnesota
11th Missouri
8th Wisconsin

THIRD BRIGADE
Brig. Gen. Charles L. Matthies
Col. Joseph J. Woods
8th Iowa
12th Iowa
35th Iowa

ARTILLERY
Capt. Nelson T. Spoor
1st Illinois Light Artillery, Battery E
2nd Battery Iowa Light Artillery

UNATTACHED CAVALRY
4th Iowa

SIXTEENTH CORPS
Maj. Gen. Stephen A. Hurlbut (posted in Memphis)

Maj. Gen. Cadwallader C. Washburn (commanding
W. Smith and Kimball)

FIRST DIVISION
Brig. Gen. William "Sooy" Smith

FIRST BRIGADE
    Col. John M. Loomis
    26th Illinois
    90th Illinois
    12th Indiana
    100th Indiana

SECOND BRIGADE
    Col. Stephen G. Hicks
    40th Illinois
    103rd Illinois
    15th Michigan
    46th Ohio

THIRD BRIGADE
    Col. Joseph R. Cockerill
    97th Indiana
    99th Indiana
    53rd Ohio
    70th Ohio

FOURTH BRIGADE
    Col. William W. Sanford
    48th Illinois
    6th Iowa

ARTILLERY
    Capt. William Cogswell
    1st Illinois Light Artillery, Battery F
    1st Illinois Light Artillery, Battery I
    Cogswell's Illinois Battery
    6th Indiana Battery

FOURTH DIVISION
    Brig. Gen. Jacob G. Lauman

FIRST BRIGADE
    Col. Isaac C. Pugh
    41st Illinois
    53rd Illinois
    3rd Iowa
    33rd Wisconsin

SECOND BRIGADE
    Col. Cyrus Hall
    14th Illinois
    15th Illinois
    46th Illinois
    76th Illinois
    53rd Indiana

THIRD BRIGADE
    Col. George E. Bryant
    Col. Amory K. Johnson
    28th Illinois
    32nd Illinois
    12th Wisconsin

ARTILLERY
    Capt. George C. Gumbart
    2nd Illinois Light Artillery, Battery E
    2nd Illinois Light Artillery, Battery K
    5th Battery Ohio Light Artillery
    7th Battery Ohio Light Artillery
    15th Battery Ohio Light Artillery

CAVALRY
    15th Illinois, Companies F and I

PROVISIONAL DIVISION
    Brig. Gen. Nathan Kimball

ENGELMANN'S BRIGADE
    Col. Adolph Engelmann
    43rd Illinois
    61st Illinois
    106th Illinois
    12th Michigan

RICHMOND'S BRIGADE
    Col. Jonathan Richmond
    18th Illinois
    54th Illinois
    126th Illinois
    22nd Ohio

MONTGOMERY'S BRIGADE
    Col. Milton Montgomery

40th Iowa
3rd Minnesota
25th Wisconsin
27th Wisconsin

SEVENTEENTH CORPS
Maj. Gen. James B. McPherson

Escort
4th Company, Ohio Cavalry

THIRD DIVISION
Maj. Gen. John A. Logan

Escort
2nd Illinois Cavalry, Company A

First Brigade
Brig. Gen. John E. Smith
Brig. Gen. Mortimer D. Leggett
20th Illinois
31st Illinois
45th Illinois
124th Illinois
23rd Indiana

Second Brigade
Brig. Gen. Mortimer D. Leggett
Col. Manning F. Force
30th Illinois
20th Ohio
68th Ohio
78th Ohio

Third Brigade
Brig. Gen. John D. Stevenson
8th Illinois
17th Illinois
81st Illinois
7th Missouri
32nd Ohio

Artillery
Maj. Charles J. Stolbrand

1st Illinois Light Artillery, Battery D
2nd Illinois Light Artillery, Battery G
2nd Illinois Light Artillery, Battery L
8th Battery Michigan Light Artillery
3rd Battery Ohio Light Artillery

SIXTH DIVISION
Brig. Gen. John McArthur

ESCORT
11th Illinois Cavalry, Company G

SECOND BRIGADE
Brig. Gen. Thomas E. G. Ransom
11th Illinois
72nd Illinois
95th Illinois
14th Wisconsin
17th Wisconsin

THIRD BRIGADE
Col. William Hall
Col. Alexander Chambers
11th Iowa
13th Iowa
15th Iowa
16th Iowa
63rd Illinois
87th Illinois

ARTILLERY
Maj. Thomas D. Maurice
2nd Illinois Light Artillery, Battery F
1st Battery Minnesota Light Artillery
1st Missouri Light Artillery, Battery C
10th Battery Ohio Light Artillery

SEVENTH DIVISION
Brig. Gen. Isaac F. Quimby
Brig. Gen. John E. Smith

ESCORT
4th Missouri Cavalry, Company F

FIRST BRIGADE
    Col. John B. Sanborn
    39th Indiana
    48th Indiana
    4th Minnesota
    18th Wisconsin

SECOND BRIGADE
    Col. Samuel A. Holmes
    Col. Green B. Raum
    56th Illinois
    17th Iowa
    10th Missouri
    24th Missouri
    80th Ohio

THIRD BRIGADE
    Col. Holden Putman
    Brig. Gen. Charles Matthies
    93rd Illinois
    5th Iowa
    10th Iowa
    26th Missouri

ARTILLERY
    Capt. Frank C. Sands
    Capt. Henry Dillon
    1st Missouri Light Artillery, Battery M
    11th Battery Ohio Light Artillery
    6th Battery Wisconsin Light Artillery
    12th Battery Wisconsin Light Artillery

UNATTACHED CAVALRY
    Col. Cyrus Bussey
    5th Illinois
    3rd Iowa
    2nd Wisconsin

APPENDIX III

CONFEDERATE ORDER OF BATTLE[1]

ARMY OF MISSISSIPPI AND EAST LOUISIANA
Lieut. Gen. John C. Pemberton

STEVENSON'S DIVISION
Maj. Gen. Carter L. Stevenson

FIRST BRIGADE
Brig. Gen. Seth M. Barton
40th Georgia
41st Georgia
42nd Georgia
43rd Georgia
52nd Georgia
Hudson's Mississippi Battery
Pointe Coupee Louisiana Artillery, Company A (section)
Pointe Coupee Louisiana Artillery, Company C

SECOND BRIGADE
Brig. Gen. Alfred Cumming
34th Georgia
36th Georgia
39th Georgia
56th Georgia

57th Georgia
Cherokee (Georgia) Artillery

THIRD BRIGADE
Brig. Gen. Stephen D. Lee
20th Alabama
23rd Alabama
30th Alabama
31st Alabama
46th Alabama
Waddell's Alabama Battery

FOURTH BRIGADE
Col. Alexander W. Reynolds
3rd Tennessee (Provisional Army)
39th Tennessee
43rd Tennessee
59th Tennessee
3rd Maryland Battery

ATTACHED
Waul's Texas Legion
1st Tennessee Cavalry (Carter's)
Botetourt Virginia Artillery
Signal Corps

FORNEY'S DIVISION
Maj. Gen. John H. Forney

FIRST BRIGADE
Brig. Gen. Louis Hebert
3rd Louisiana
21st Louisiana
36th Mississippi
37th Mississippi
38th Mississippi
43rd Mississippi
7th Mississippi Battalion
2nd Alabama Artillery Battalion, Company C
Appeal Arkansas Battery

SECOND BRIGADE
Brig. Gen. John C. Moore

37th Alabama
40th Alabama
42nd Alabama
35th Mississippi
40th Mississippi
2nd Texas
Sengstak's Alabama Battery
Pointe Coupee Louisiana Artillery, Company B

SMITH'S DIVISION
Maj. Gen. Martin L. Smith

BALDWIN'S BRIGADE
Brig. Gen. William E. Baldwin
17th Louisiana
31st Louisiana
4th Mississippi
46th Mississippi
Tobin's Tennessee Battery

SHOUP'S BRIGADE
Brig. Gen. Francis A. Shoup
26th Louisiana
27th Louisiana
29th Louisiana
McNally's Battery

VAUGHN'S BRIGADE
Brig. Gen. John C. Vaughn
60th Tennessee
61st Tennessee
62nd Tennessee

MISSISSIPPI STATE TROOPS (commanded by Vaughan)
Brig. Gen. Jeptha V. Harris
5th Regiment Minute Men
3rd Battalion Minute Men

ATTACHED
14th Mississippi Light Artillery Battery
Mississippi Partisan Rangers
Signal Corps

BOWEN'S DIVISION
Maj. Gen. John S. Bowen

FIRST BRIGADE
Col. Francis M. Cockrell
1st Missouri
2nd Missouri
3rd Missouri
5th Missouri
6th Missouri
Guibor's Missouri Battery
Landis's Missouri Battery
Wade's Missouri Battery

SECOND BRIGADE
Brig. Gen. Martin E. Green
Col. Thomas P. Dockery
19th Arkansas
20th Arkansas
1st Arkansas Cavalry Battalion
12th Arkansas Battalion of Sharpshooters
1st Missouri Cavalry
3rd Missouri Cavalry
3rd Missouri Battery
Lowe's Missouri Battery

RIVER DEFENSES (BATTERIES)
Col. Edward Higgins
1st Louisiana Heavy Artillery
8th Louisiana Heavy Artillery Battalion
21st Louisiana
1st Mississippi Light Artillery, Company L
1st Tennessee Heavy Artillery
Caruthers's Tennessee Battery
Johnston's Tennessee Battery
Lynch's Tennessee Battery
Vaiden's Mississippi Battery

MISCELLANEOUS
54th Alabama (detachment)

City Guards

Signal Corps

ARMY OF RELIEF
Gen. Joseph E. Johnston

BRECKINRIDGE'S DIVISION
Maj. Gen. John C. Breckinridge

GIBSON'S BRIGADE
Col. Randall L. Gibson

32nd Alabama

13th/20th Louisiana

16th/25th Louisiana

19th Louisiana

14th Louisiana Battalion of Sharpshooters

HELM'S BRIGADE
Brig. Gen. Benjamin H. Helm

41st Alabama

2nd Kentucky

4th Kentucky

6th Kentucky

9th Kentucky

STOVALL'S BRIGADE
Brig. Gen. Marcellus A. Stovall

1st/3rd Florida

4th Florida

47th Georgia

60th North Carolina

ARTILLERY
Maj. Rice E. Graves

Johnston's Tennessee Battery

Cobb's Kentucky Battery

Washington Louisiana Artillery, 5th Company

FRENCH'S DIVISION
Maj. Gen. Samuel G. French

McNair's Brigade
  Brig. Gen. Evander McNair
  1st Arkansas Mounted Rifles
  2nd Arkansas Mounted Rifles
  4th Arkansas
  25th/31st Arkansas
  39th North Carolina

Maxey's Brigade
  Brig. Gen. Samuel B. Maxey
  4th Louisiana
  30th Louisiana
  42nd Tennessee
  46th/55th Tennessee
  48th Tennessee
  49th Tennessee
  53rd Tennessee
  1st Texas Battalion of Sharpshooters

Evans's Brigade
  Brig. Gen. Nathan G. Evans
  17th South Carolina
  18th South Carolina
  22nd South Carolina
  23rd South Carolina
  26th South Carolina
  Holcombe Legion

Artillery
  Fenner's Louisiana Battery
  Palmetto South Carolina Artillery, Company B
  Palmetto South Carolina Artillery, Company C

LORING'S DIVISION (originally attached to Pemberton)
  Maj. Gen. William W. Loring

First Brigade
  Brig. Gen. John Adams
  1st Confederate Battalion
  6th Mississippi
  15th Mississippi
  20th Mississippi

23rd Mississippi
26th Mississippi
Culbertson's Mississippi Battery
Cowan's Mississippi Battery

SECOND BRIGADE
Brig. Gen. Winfield S. Featherston
3rd Mississippi
22nd Mississippi
31st Mississippi
33rd Mississippi
1st Mississippi Battalion of Sharpshooters
Charpentier's Alabama Battery
Wofford's Mississippi Battery

THIRD BRIGADE
Brig. Gen. Abraham Buford
27th Alabama
35th Alabama
54th Alabama
55th Alabama
9th Arkansas
3rd Kentucky
7th Kentucky
8th Kentucky
12th Louisiana
3rd Missouri Cavalry (dismounted)
Pointe Coupee Louisiana Artillery, Company C (4 guns)
Lookout Tennessee Artillery

WALKER'S DIVISION
Maj. Gen. William H. T. Walker

ESCORT
Nelson's Independent Georgia Calvary Company

ECTOR'S BRIGADE
Brig. Gen. Matthew D. Ector
9th Texas
10th Texas Cavalry (dismounted)
14th Texas Cavalry (dismounted)
32nd Texas Cavalry (dismounted)

Alabama Battalion of Sharpshooters
Mississippi Battalion of Sharpshooters
McNally's Arkansas Battery

GREGG'S BRIGADE
Brig. Gen. John Gregg
3rd Tennessee
10th Tennessee
30th Tennessee
41st Tennessee
50th Tennessee
1st Tennessee Battalion
7th Texas
14th Mississippi
Bledsoe's Missouri Battery

GIST'S BRIGADE
Brig. Gen. States Rights Gist
46th Georgia
8th Georgia Battalion
16th South Carolina
24th South Carolina
Ferguson's South Carolina Battery

WILSON'S BRIGADE
Col. Claudius C. Wilson
25th Georgia
29th Georgia
30th Georgia
1st Georgia Battalion of Sharpshooters
4th Louisiana Battalion
Martin's Georgia Battery

JACKSON'S CAVALRY DIVISION
Brig. Gen. William H. Jackson

FIRST BRIGADE
Brig. Gen. George B. Cosby
1st Mississippi Cavalry
4th Mississippi Cavalry
28th Mississippi Cavalry
Wirt Adams's Mississippi Cavalry

Ballentine's Mississippi Cavalry
17th Mississippi Battalion
Clark's Missouri Artillery

SECOND BRIGADE
Brig. Gen. John G. Whitfield
3rd Texas Cavalry
6th Texas Cavalry
9th Texas Cavalry
1st Texas Legion
Bridges's Arkansas Battalion

ESCORTS AND GUARDS
Company A, 7th Tennessee Cavalry
Independent Company, Louisiana Cavalry
Provost Guard

RESERVE ARTILLERY
Columbus Georgia Battery
Durrive's Louisiana Battery

APPENDIX IV

REINFORCING VICKSBURG

While Maj. Gen. Ulysses S. Grant was busy first attempting to work his way to Vicksburg and then deciding to bypass the city, the Confederate high command took several important actions and made significant commitments. Pres. Jefferson Davis made a critical decision regarding the Gettysburg Campaign that held great ramifications for Vicksburg and its commander, Lieut. Gen. John C. Pemberton. Most likely this critical decision came too late to be of assistance to Pemberton, but we need to review it.[1]

Why don't we discuss this critical decision as another one in the series pertaining to Vicksburg? Technically, the choice was not pertinent to the Vicksburg Campaign. We must remember what we have accepted as the definition of a critical decision in the Command Decisions in America's Civil War series, as noted in the preface. We specifically define a critical decision as one of such importance that it shaped not only the events immediately following it, but also the events from that point forward throughout a battle or campaign. On or about May 15, 1863, after an all-day meeting, Davis opted to support Gen. Robert E. Lee's proposed invasion of Pennsylvania. Therefore, by supporting Lee, Davis declined to remove any part of the general's command to send it west to reinforce Pemberton/Johnston. Note that this was a Gettysburg Campaign critical decision, not a Vicksburg Campaign critical decision. Simply put, Davis sent no additional troops from Lee's Command to provide assistance, and in doing so, the Confederate president did not change the outcome of the fighting for Vicksburg. Therefore, in accordance with the definition above, this action was not a critical decision directly affecting the Vicksburg Campaign! Nonetheless, this situation deserves more consideration.[2]

President Davis was certainly cognizant of the vulnerability of Vicksburg (and Port Hudson), which had been a major Federal target since the beginning of the war, with general-in-chief Winfield Scott's proposed Anaconda Plan. Upon appointment to department command, Grant attempted to capture Vicksburg, initially advancing south along the Mississippi Central Railroad in December 1862. Therefore, on December 14, Davis ordered some eleven thousand troops commanded by Maj. Gen. Carter Stevenson, Brig. Gen. Samuel B. Maxey, and Maj. Gen. Franklin Gardner to leave Gen. Braxton Bragg's Army of Tennessee in Middle Tennessee. These troops were to report to Pemberton, commanding the Department of Mississippi and East Louisiana, including Vicksburg. (The timing of this order was particularly detrimental to Bragg, as he lost a quarter of his army just days before the unexpected Battle of Stones River, beginning on December 31. How might the outcome have changed with these additional soldiers present?) Yet beyond this support Davis sent few additional troops. Maj. Gen. Earl Van Dorn's raid on Grant's supply depot at Holly Springs on December 20 ruined the Union commander's initial attempt to reach Vicksburg from the north. Maj. Gen. William T. Sherman's defeat at the Battle of Chickasaw Bayou from December 26 to December 29 certainly sustained Confederate confidence in their defense of the city.[3]

After these defeats and Grant's four additional failures to successfully advance on Vicksburg from above or beside it, apparently both Davis and Pemberton somewhat relaxed their vigilance. Rear Adm. David D. Porter's successful run past the Vicksburg batteries during the night of April 16, 1863, with gunboats, transports, and barges, Col. Benjamin Grierson's late April raid south through the heart of Mississippi, and Col. Abel Streight's raid east into Alabama stirred Confederate awareness of new Federal activity around the river city confusing Pemberton. Yet only when Grant successfully marched down the west bank of the Mississippi and crossed over with his command to Bruinsburg on April 30 did Confederates' concern really mount. Also on the thirtieth, Sherman's decoy assault on Snyder's Bluff added to the confusion. By then, as we will see, it was already too late for reinforcements to be of any major assistance to Pemberton. Grant's blitzkrieg, including the Battles of Port Gibson, Raymond, Jackson, Champion Hill, and Big Black River Bridge, resulted in Pemberton's Command being bottled up within Vicksburg on May 18. After failed assaults on the nineteenth and twenty-second, Grant settled down to siege operations.[4]

Back on November 24, 1862, Davis assigned Gen. Joseph E. Johnston command of most of the Western Theater. Still recovering from his wounds at Seven Pines, or Fair Oaks, the officer nonetheless proceeded into the theater. However, for reasons inexplicable to the Confederate president, Johnston refused to accept responsibility for directing his two principal armies: Gen. Braxton Bragg's Army of Tennessee, and Pemberton's Army of Vicksburg. It seemed that wherever he went during the war, Johnston called for reinforcements, even when told repeatedly they were unavailable. However, Davis bore the responsibility to decide which army and state deserved Johnston's undivided attention, but the president failed to accept it.[5]

Apparently, Davis had long been considering ordering reinforcements, particularly from Lee's Army of Northern Virginia, to aid Pemberton. We can begin by examining correspondence from Lee to Davis on April 16 in which Lee believed it better to maintain aggressiveness. Based on the various relevant primary and secondary sources, Lee seemed, most reasonably, to want to keep his army intact and to advance into Pennsylvania. He maintained that these objectives would largely reduce the Confederacy's dependence on Virginia and Tennessee farmers, allowing his army to live off the enemy's land for a change. In addition, Lee thought that keeping his force together and headed for Pennsylvania would allow his men to give battle and score a great military victory. This success could also change foreign and Federal opinion, which currently failed to recognize the Confederacy as an independent country.[6]

President Davis had to quickly decide whether he could afford to send reinforcements to either Pemberton or Johnston. If he could do so, from what command or commands would he procure them? In the meantime, Grant maneuvered south of Vicksburg, crossed the Mississippi River to Bruinsburg, and advanced northeast, intent on first stripping the state capital at Jackson of the ability to supply Pemberton and Johnston's commands. After a small battle at Raymond on May 12, the Federal commander succeeded in capturing Jackson on May 14, destroying anything of military value. He then marched west, wrecking the Southern Railroad supplying Vicksburg from Jackson. Obviously, Vicksburg itself was now Grant's immediate objective.[7]

During Grant's maneuvers, as noted in chapter 5, Davis issued orders (via Secretary of War James Seddon) on May 9 for Johnston to assist Pemberton. Johnston arrived at Jackson on May 13, stating, "I am too late." His words implied that there was nothing he might do without reinforcements.[8]

Meanwhile, both Davis's and Lee's attention was diverted to halting the sudden advance toward Richmond by new commander of the Federal Army of the Potomac Maj. Gen. Joseph Hooker. Lee's resounding victory (although at the cost of significant casualties) at the Battle of Chancellorsville from April 30 to May 6 resulted in Hooker's retreat. This further enticed Lee to advance into Pennsylvania. He continued to press for permission to invade the state.[9]

The defining event concerning reinforcements was a meeting held in Richmond on May 15 and attended by Davis, Lee, and Secretary of War James A. Seddon. This meeting lasted all day, as noted by clerk John B. Jones. Unfortunately, no record of this gathering exists, forcing historians to make assumptions as to what transpired. However, we can conclude that Lee successfully defended his plan to invade Pennsylvania. History supports this view, for the Confederate president held another meeting on the subject the following day, this time with his full cabinet in attendance. The only available record of this meeting available is that of Postmaster General John H. Reagan, who remembered the decision to support Lee and his proposed northern invasion. However, as Jones noted on May 16, the sight of Maj. Gen. George Pickett's division marching through Richmond that day and heading to Lee's camp strongly suggested that the choice had been made the prior day (the fifteenth). Lee had successfully convinced his president of the viability of his desired campaign north.[10]

This decision to support Lee had several important ramifications. The Confederate commander desired to confront the Federal Army of the Potomac and defeat it. First, of course, the pursuit of this goal led to the Gettysburg Campaign and the resulting battle. The largest engagement of the Civil War, the Battle of Gettysburg handed Lee his largest major defeat, forcing him to retreat out of Pennsylvania. By the end of the campaign he had suffered some 27,125 casualties, and he had generally been forced to take the defensive for the remainder of the war. Likewise, foreign support of the Confederacy largely evaporated. Of course, the failure to further reinforce Pemberton, Johnston, or both officers directly led to Grant successfully capturing Vicksburg after a forty-seven-day siege. We will never know for sure what influence, if any, these reinforcements might have had on the outcome of the fighting. However, because of Davis's decision to support Lee, the Confederacy certainly helped Grant maintain his siege and ultimately compel the surrender of this impediment to Federal river traffic (and Port Hudson).[11]

Taking this decision a step further, in an analysis similar to our discussion of alternate scenarios for critical decisions, what if Davis had sent reinforcements to Pemberton or Johnston? First, in the Eastern Theater Lee would have likely lost about a third of his army, potentially Lieut. Gen. James Longstreet's corps, as it traveled west to provide relief to Vicksburg. Longstreet's Corps was the reasonable choice for this assignment, as the officer had lobbied for the opportunity to go west in support of the western armies. This loss of combat power would have forced Lee to postpone or cancel his proposed invasion of Pennsylvania, and remain on the defense protecting Richmond. The huge significance of not moving north would have resulted in no Battle of Gettysburg, and no critical defeat and heavy loss of soldiers for Lee's army. If and when Longstreet, or whoever, and his command returned to Lee, assuming the force was still largely intact, Lee might then have tried advancing north again, possibly with a better outcome.[12]

What effect might the dispatch of Longstreet's Corps (or another similar one) have had on the outcome of the Vicksburg Campaign? Had Davis decided to send reinforcements to Pemberton early in 1863, would Pemberton have employed them any better? Since the final decision to provide help apparently wasn't made until May 15, by the time the additional troops would have arrived, Vicksburg was already under siege. Therefore, these reinforcements would have reported to Johnston. Would he have been any more assertive? His past performance indicated a distaste for aggressive movements. All indications point to Johnston denying any chance to break Pemberton's Command out of the city, and he appeared simply to pretend to maneuver without seriously expecting positive results. With Maj. Gen. William T. Sherman commanding a line of troops protecting the siege line (a line of contravallation), even if assaulted by a reinforced Johnston, Grant would have been able to supply additional soldiers to support Sherman.[13]

Perhaps even more important, how much time would it have taken to get rebel reinforcements that far west? While Chattanooga remained under Confederate control, the railroads leading west from the city were not all functional. A considerable amount of marching might be required between operating lines, and Grant had also destroyed the railroad from Jackson to Vicksburg. All in all, had Davis sent Johnston reinforcements, they would have been unlikely to significantly change the situation, even if they had arrived in reasonable time.[14]

The problem with this possibility is the timing. When we move into alternate scenarios we must be extremely careful to extrapolate events as realistically as possible. Immediately after the Battle of Chickamauga, the Federal movement of the Eleventh of Twelfth Corps from Virginia to Chattanooga began within twenty-four hours of the decision to undertake it. In a similar future action, once Davis decided to send two divisions of Lieut. Gen. James Longstreet's corps plus some artillery to reinforce Bragg near Chattanooga, the Confederates took almost two weeks in preparation before the initial troops boarded trains for that city. This would place their departure near the end of May. By May 18, Grant had won the Battles of Champion Hill and Big Black River Bridge and forced Pemberton into the Vicksburg defenses. After assaults on May 19 and May 22, the Federal commander had already established the siege.[15]

It is beyond the scope of this brief description of possible events to delve into the railroad problems of the Confederacy. However, it would likely have taken at least several weeks traveling via the railroads and riverboats and marching between gaps in the railroads for this relief force to arrive in the area. At this time the Confederates still controlled Chattanooga. Direct service from Richmond to Chattanooga entailed 540 miles, which nominally took four days to cover. From Chattanooga the only through railroad service went in reverse of Bragg's initial use of the railroad. When the rebel general departed Tupelo in late July 1862, reaching Chattanooga required a trip of some 776 miles via six different railroads and a short ferry ride across Mobile Bay. This movement took a minimum of six days. Changing the last leg of the journey from Mobile to Jackson instead of Tupelo would save roughly fifty miles. This then required around 1,266 miles of railroad travel.[16]

Grant had also destroyed the railroad west of Jackson. Remember that changes of trains were required due to differences in the tracks' gauge. In addition, two more years of wear and tear on the line would significantly prolong travel times due to the slower speeds trains had to maintain in order to avoid derailments. Even accepting the best possibility of requiring only ten days to make the trip to Chattanooga and providing rations for the troops, the Confederates would arrive without supply wagons or rations for upcoming deployment. Under ideal circumstances, in which troops left a few days after May 15, the earliest possible arrival at Jackson would have been around the twenty-seventh, with Grant's siege already established and additional reinforcements en route.[17]

Had Johnston changed his defensive mindset and assaulted Grant's line, he would have found it well fortified and eventually protected by Sherman's line of contravallation. Even being most optimistic about the possibility of Johnston breaking into the Confederate defensive line surrounding Vicksburg, as the half-starved soldiers would flee, Grant's troops would quickly capture the city and likely force the surrender of both Confederate armies. Additional considerations would have been the lack of supply wagons, as well as the ability to provide provisions for this command, similar to Longstreet's situation upon arrival for the Battle of Chickamauga. Johnston himself indicated that he could not maneuver more than four days away from a railroad supply line.[18]

Based on all of the above concerns, had Davis dispatched reinforcements to Vicksburg immediately after his meeting with Lee on May 15, it is logical to conclude that they would have been too little, too late, even under the best of circumstances. Extra support for the Confederates would not have changed the outcome of Grant's siege.[19]

NOTES

Introduction

1. James M. McPherson, *Battle Cry of Freedom: The Civil War Era* (New York: Ballantine Books, 1988), 254, 264, 273–74.

2. McPherson, *Battle Cry of Freedom*, 274.

3. McPherson, *Battle Cry of Freedom*, 339–50.

4. Ezra J. Warner, *Generals in Blue: Lives of the Union Commanders* (Baton Rouge: Louisiana State University Press, 1964), 290–92.

5. McPherson, *Battle Cry of Freedom*, 461–62.

6. McPherson, *Battle Cry of Freedom*, 536–45, 555–57.

7. Warner, *Generals in Blue*, 376–77.

8. Michael A. Palmer, *Lee Moves North: Robert E. Lee on the Offensive* (New York: John Wiley and Sons, 1998), 48–49.

9. McPherson, *Battle Cry of Freedom*, 652–55.

10. McPherson, *Battle Cry of Freedom*, 653–63.

11. Jeffrey L. Patrick, *Campaign for Wilson's Creek: The Fight for Missouri Begins* (Buffalo Gap, TX: McWhiney Foundation Press, 2011), 129–87.

12. Alvin M. Joseph, *The Civil War in the American West* (New York: Vintage Books, 1991), 319–46.

13. Joseph, *Civil War in the American West*, 61–92.

14. Joseph, *Civil War in the American West*, 363–67.

15. Michael B. Ballard, *Vicksburg: The Campaign That Opened the Mississippi* (Chapel Hill: University of North Carolina Press, 2004), 14–17.

16. Thomas L. Connelly, *Army of the Heartland: The Army of Tennessee, 1861–1862* (Baton Rouge: Louisiana State University Press, 1967), 4–9.

17. Nathaniel C. Hughes Jr., *The Battle of Belmont: Grant Strikes South* (Chapel Hill: University of North Carolina Press, 1991), 1–5.

18. McPherson, *Battle Cry of Freedom*, 333-34.

19. Warner, *Generals in Blue*, 184.

20. Hughes, *Battle of Belmont*, 53–77, 207–8.

21. Timothy B. Smith, *Grant Invades Tennessee: The 1862 Battles for Forts Henry and Donelson* (Lawrence: University Press of Kansas, 2016), 51, 66–67, 155.

22. Kenneth A. Hafendorfer, *Mill Springs: Campaign and Battle of Mill Springs, Kentucky* (Louisville: KH Press, 2010), 181–212; Smith, *Grant Invades Tennessee*, 133, 353–64.

23. Timothy B. Smith, *Shiloh: Conquer or Perish* (Lawrence: University Press of Kansas, 2014), 51–52, 94–105, 392–95.

24. Smith, *Shiloh: Conquer or Perish*, 416–17.

25. Timothy B. Smith, *The Decision Was Always My Own: Ulysses S. Grant and the Vicksburg Campaign* (Carbondale: Southern Illinois University Press, 2018), 6–8.

Chapter 1. Before the Vicksburg Campaign Begins

1. Ballard, *Vicksburg*, 1; Wikipedia, s.v., "Mississippi," accessed December 27, 2021, https://en.wikipedia.org/wiki/Mississippi.

2. Ballard, *Vicksburg*, 38, 50–53, 168, 199. Of the thirty-seven large-caliber cannon, seventeen were rifled while twenty were smoothbores.

3. Lawrence L. Hewitt, "The Struggle for Port Hudson, Louisiana," *Blue & Gray Magazine* 28, no. 1 (2011), 6–7; McPherson, *Battle Cry of Freedom*, 333–34, 637.

4. Larry J. Daniel, *Days of Glory: The Army of the Cumberland, 1861–1865* (Baton Rouge: Louisiana State University Press, 2004), 85–87.

5. US War Department, *The War of the Rebellion: A Compilation of the Official Records of the Union and Confederate Armies* (Washington, DC: US

Government Printing Office, 1880–1901), vol. 17, pt. 2, p. 150. Hereafter, this source is cited in the following format: *OR*, vol. 17, pt. 2, p. 150. All references are to series 1 unless otherwise noted. Ulysses S. Grant, *Personal Memoirs of U. S. Grant, in Two Volumes* (1885; repr., Harrisburg, PA: Archive Society, 1997), 1:393–419; Ballard, *Vicksburg*, 70–78; McPherson, *Battle Cry of Freedom*, 522–23.

6. Ballard, *Vicksburg*, 76–78; Ezra J. Warner, *Generals in Gray: Lives of the Confederate Commanders* (Baton Rouge: Louisiana State University Press, 1959), 315; McPherson, *Battle Cry of Freedom*, 522–23.

7. McPherson, *Battle Cry of Freedom*, 576; Warner, *Generals in Gray*, 22–23.

8. Warner, *Generals in Gray*, 232–33; Ballard, *Vicksburg*, 86; McPherson, *Battle Cry of Freedom*, 576.

9. Warner, *Generals in Gray*, 232–33; Ballard, *Vicksburg*, 86; McPherson, *Battle Cry of Freedom*, 576; Michael B. Ballard, *Pemberton: A Biography* (Jackson: University Press of Mississippi, 1991), 96–102.

10. Warner, *Generals in Gray*, 161–62; McPherson, *Battle Cry of Freedom*, 576.

11. Warner, *Generals in Gray*, 22–23; McPherson, *Battle Cry of Freedom*, 365–66.

12. Larry Peterson, *Decisions of the 1862 Kentucky Campaign: The Twenty-Seven Critical Decisions That Defined the Operation* (Knoxville: University of Tennessee Press, 2019), 43–50, 81–87.

13. *OR*, vol. 17, pt. 2, p. 820; Warner, *Generals in Gray*, 232–33; McPherson, *Battle Cry of Freedom*, 576.

14. *OR*, vol. 17, pt. 2, pp. 724, 726–28; Warner, *Generals in Gray*, 232; McPherson, *Battle Cry of Freedom*, 576.

15. Author's conjecture.

16. Grant, *Personal Memoirs*, 1:385; Lloyd Lewis, *Sherman: Fighting Prophet* (New York: Konecky and Konecky, 1932), 235–36.

17. Grant, *Personal Memoirs*, 1:393–96.

18. Grant, *Personal Memoirs*, 1:420–21; William S. McFeely, *Grant: A Biography* (New York: W. W. Norton, 1981), 121–23.

19. Warner, *Generals in Blue*, 183–84; McFeely, *Grant: A Biography*, 122.

20. Warner, *Generals in Blue*, 293; McPherson, *Battle Cry of Freedom*, 328–29; Ballard, *Vicksburg*, 80.

21. *OR*, vol. 17, pt. 2, p. 294; Grant, *Personal Memoirs*, 1:421.

22. *OR*, vol. 17, pt. 2, pp. 274–75, 282; Ballard, *Vicksburg*, 80–81.

23. William T. Sherman, *Memoirs of General Sherman, by Himself, in Two Volumes* (1875; repr., Harrisburg, PA: Archive Society, 1997), 1:334; Lewis, *Sherman: Fighting Prophet*, 292.

24. *OR*, vol. 13, pp. 906–7; Steven E. Woodworth, *Jefferson Davis and His Generals: The Failure of Confederate Command in the West* (Lawrence: University Press of Kansas, 1990), 180.

25. *OR*, vol. 13, pp. 906–7; Woodworth, *Jefferson Davis and His Generals*, 180.

26. Ballard, *Pemberton*, 119–20; Woodworth, *Jefferson Davis and His Generals*, 180; Ballard, *Vicksburg*, 116–18.

27. Ballard, *Pemberton*, 119–20; Woodworth, *Jefferson Davis and His Generals*, 180; Ballard, *Vicksburg*, 116–18.

28. Ballard, *Pemberton*, 119–20; Woodworth, *Jefferson Davis and His Generals*, 180; Ballard, *Vicksburg*, 116–18.

29. Ballard, *Pemberton*, 119–20; Woodworth, *Jefferson Davis and His Generals*, 180; Ballard, *Vicksburg*, 116–18.

30. Ballard, *Pemberton*, 119–20; Woodworth, *Jefferson Davis and His Generals*, 180; Ballard, *Vicksburg*, 116–18.

31. Ballard, *Pemberton*, 119–20; Woodworth, *Jefferson Davis and His Generals*, 180; Ballard, *Vicksburg*, 116–18. Randolph was replaced by James A. Seddon, who served as Confederate secretary of war from November 21, 1862, until February 5, 1865.

32. *OR*, vol. 17, pt. 2, pp. 757, 763, 767–68, 771, 786; Ballard, *Pemberton*, 119–20; Woodworth, *Jefferson Davis and His Generals*, 93–94, 204, 220.

33. Author's conjecture.

Chapter 2. Grant Advances South through Central Mississippi

1. Terrence J. Winschel, *Triumph & Defeat: The Vicksburg Campaign* (New York: Savas Beatie, 2004), 1:5–6, 8; Steven E. Woodworth and Charles D. Grear, eds., *The Vicksburg Campaign: March 29–May 18, 1863* (Carbondale: Southern Illinois University Press, 2013), 1–2.

2. Winschel, *Triumph & Defeat*, 1:5–6, 8; Woodworth and Grear, *Vicksburg Campaign*, 1–2.

3. Ballard, *Vicksburg*, 54–55.

4. McPherson, *Battle Cry of Freedom*, 579; Ballard, *Vicksburg*, 111.

5. McPherson, *Battle Cry of Freedom*, 577; Woodworth and Grear, *Vicksburg Campaign*, 1.

6. *OR*, vol. 17, pt. 2, pp. 296, 347–48, 362–63; *OR*, vol. 17, pt. 1, p. 469; Grant, *Personal Memoirs*, 1:422–24; Winschel, *Triumph & Defeat*, 1:5–6; McPherson, *Battle Cry of Freedom*, 577; Ballard, *Vicksburg*, 81. See also maps on pp. 10–11 in Thomas E. Parson, "Thwarting Grant's First Drive on Vicksburg: Van Dorn's Holly Springs Raid," *Blue & Gray Magazine* 17, no. 3 (2010); Edwin C. Bearss, *The Vicksburg Campaign*, vol. 1, *Vicksburg Is the Key* (Dayton, OH: Morningside House, 1985), 32; Smith, *Decision Was Always My Own*, 7–9.

7. *OR*, vol. 17, pt. 1, pp. 474, 601; Grant, *Personal Memoirs*, 1:430–31; William T. Sherman, *Memoirs of General William T. Sherman* (1875; repr., Harrisburg, PA: Archive Society, 1997), 1:281–83; Bearss, *Vicksburg Campaign*, 1:59, 71; Ballard, *Vicksburg*, 111.

8. *OR*, vol. 17, pt. 1, pp. 474, 601; Grant, *Personal Memoirs*, 1:430–31; Sherman, *Memoirs*, 1:281–83; Bearss, *Vicksburg Campaign*, 1:59, 71; Ballard, *Vicksburg*, 111.

9. Ballard, *Vicksburg*, 111–12.

10. Ballard, *Vicksburg*, 132–33.

11. Grant, *Personal Memoirs*, 1:430–31; *OR*, vol. 17, pt. 1, p. 613. For a detailed description of the Chickasaw Bayou Campaign, see Terrence J. Winschel, "Chickasaw Bayou: Sherman's Winter of Despair," *Blue & Gray Magazine* 16, no. 3 (2009).

12. Grant, *Personal Memoirs*, 1:430–31; Parson, "Thwarting Grant's First Drive on Vicksburg;" Winschel, "Chickasaw Bayou," 6, 10; Ballard, *Vicksburg*, 103–4.

13. Ballard, *Pemberton*, 125-27; Ballard, *Vicksburg*, 117, 121.

14. Ballard, *Pemberton*, 125-27; Ballard, *Vicksburg*, 117, 121.

15. Ballard, *Pemberton*, 125-27; Ballard, *Vicksburg*, 117, 121.

16. Ballard, *Vicksburg*, 121; Parson, "Thwarting Grant's First Drive on Vicksburg," 6–7.

17. Parson, "Thwarting Grant's First Drive on Vicksburg," 8–9, 12 (map); Ballard, *Pemberton*, 127; McPherson, *Battle Cry of Freedom*, 578.

18. Grant, *Personal Memoirs*, 1:433; Parson, "Thwarting Grant's First Drive on Vicksburg," 9, 11 (map), 13 (map), 19.

19. Parson, "Thwarting Grant's First Drive on Vicksburg," 12 (map), 19–20; Ballard, *Pemberton*, 127.

20. Parson, "Thwarting Grant's First Drive on Vicksburg," 14 (map), 20–24, 42–46.

21. *OR*, vol. 17, pt. 2, p. 489; Grant, *Personal Memoirs*, 1:435; Parson, "Thwarting Grant's First Drive on Vicksburg," 49–50.

22. *OR*, vol. 17, pt. 1, p. 516; Parson, "Thwarting Grant's First Drive on Vicksburg," 49.

Chapter 3. Grant Advances down the West Side of the Mississippi

1. Grant, *Personal Memoirs*, 1:445–46; McFeely, *Grant: A Biography*, 128–29; Ballard, *Vicksburg*, 156; Ballard, *Pemberton*, 132.

2. *OR*, 15, pp. 25–30; Grant, *Personal Memoirs*, 1:445–46; Warner, *Generals in Blue*, 563–64; Ballard, *Vicksburg*, 159, 171; Winschel, *Triumph & Defeat*, 1:7 (maps).

3. Grant, *Personal Memoirs*, 1:447–49; Ballard, *Vicksburg*, 173–74; Winschel, *Triumph & Defeat*, 1:7 (maps).

4. *OR*, vol. 24, pt. 1, pp. 17, 373; Grant, *Personal Memoirs*, 1:449–50; Winschel, *Triumph & Defeat*, 1:7 (maps); Ballard, *Vicksburg*, 175. Grant states in his *Personal Memoirs* that the levee was cut on February 2.

5. *OR*, vol. 24, pt. 1, pp. 17, 389–91; Grant, *Personal Memoirs*, 1:450–52; Ballard, *Vicksburg*, 174–84; Winschel, *Triumph & Defeat*, 1:7 (maps).

6. *OR*, vol. 24, pt. 3, pp. 112–13; Grant, *Personal Memoirs*, 1:452–53; Ballard, *Vicksburg*, 184–85; Winschel, *Triumph & Defeat*, 1:7 (maps).

7. *OR*, vol. 24, pt. 3, pp. 112–13; Grant, *Personal Memoirs*, 1:452–53; Ballard, *Vicksburg*, 184–85; Winschel, *Triumph & Defeat*, 1:7 (maps); J. F. C. Fuller, *The Generalship of Ulysses S. Grant* (1929; repr., New York: Da Capo, 1956), 184.

8. Grant, *Personal Memoirs*, 1:460–61; Winschel, *Triumph & Defeat*, 1:6, 8; McFeely, *Grant: A Biography*, 128–29; Edward H. Bonekemper III, *Grant and Lee: Victorious American and Vanquished Virginian* (Washington, DC: Regnery, 2012), 214.

9. Grant, *Personal Memoirs*, 1:460–61; Winschel, *Triumph & Defeat*, 1:6, 8; McFeely, *Grant: A Biography*, 128–29.

10. Grant, *Personal Memoirs*, 1:460–61; Winschel, *Triumph & Defeat*, 1:6, 8; McFeely, *Grant: A Biography*, 128–29.

11. Winschel, *Triumph & Defeat*, 1:6, 8; McFeely, *Grant: A Biography*, 128–29.

12. *OR*, vol. 24, pt. 3, p. 168; Grant, *Personal Memoirs*, 1:460–61; McFeely, *Grant: A Biography*, 128–29; Ballard, *Vicksburg*, 191; Bonekemper, *Grant and Lee*, 214.

13. *OR*, vol. 24, pt. 3, p. 168; Grant, *Personal Memoirs*, 1:460–61; McFeely, *Grant: A Biography*, 128–29; Ballard, *Vicksburg*, 191.

14. Grant, *Personal Memoirs*, 1:461; *OR*, vol. 24, pt. 1, pp. 25–26; *OR*, vol. 24, pt. 3, pp. 151–52, 168; Ballard, *Vicksburg*, 195.

15. Grant, *Personal Memoirs*, 1:461; *OR*, vol. 24, pt. 1, pp. 25–26; *OR*, vol. 24, pt. 3, pp. 151–52, 168; Ballard, *Vicksburg*, 195.

16. Grant, *Personal Memoirs*, 1:461; *OR*, vol. 24, pt. 1, pp. 25–26; *OR*, vol. 24, pt. 3, pp. 151–52, 168; Ballard, *Vicksburg*, 195.

17. Grant, *Personal Memoirs*, 1:461; *OR*, vol. 24, pt. 1, pp. 25–26; *OR*, vol. 24, pt. 3, pp. 151–52, 168; Ballard, *Vicksburg*, 195; Winschel, *Triumph & Defeat*,1:20.

18. Grant, *Personal Memoirs*, 1:461; *OR*, vol. 24, pt. 1, pp. 25–26; *OR*, vol. 24, pt. 3, pp. 151–52, 168; Ballard, *Vicksburg*, 195.

19. Grant, *Personal Memoirs*, 1:461; *OR*, vol. 24, pt. 1, pp. 25–26; *OR*, vol. 24, pt. 3, pp. 151–52, 168; Ballard, *Vicksburg*, 195.

20. Grant, *Personal Memoirs*, 1:461; Ballard, *Vicksburg*, 191.

21. Grant, *Personal Memoirs*, 1:462; Ballard, *Vicksburg*, 198.

22. Grant, *Personal Memoirs*, 1:462–64; Ballard, *Vicksburg*, 199; Gary D. Joiner, "Running the Gauntlet: The Effectiveness of Combined Forces in the Vicksburg Campaign," in Woodworth and Grear, *Vicksburg Campaign*, 13–14; Winschel, *Triumph & Defeat*, 1:25; Bearss, *Vicksburg Campaign*, 1:59.

23. Grant, *Personal Memoirs*, 1:463–64; Bearss, *Vicksburg Campaign*, 1:59–71; Joiner, "Running the Gauntlet," Woodworth and Grear, *Vicksburg Campaign*, 14–15.

24. Grant, *Personal Memoirs*, 1:471; Bearss, *Vicksburg Campaign*, 1:75–79; Joiner, "Running the Gauntlet," Woodworth and Grear, *Vicksburg Campaign*, 15–16.

25. Author's conjecture.

Chapter 4. Grant Prepares to Advance on Vicksburg

1. Bonekemper, *Grant and Lee*, 213. See Michael B. Ballard, "Grant, McClernand, and Vicksburg: A Clash of Personalities and Backgrounds,"

in Woodworth and Grear, *Vicksburg Campaign*, 129–52, for a good description of this relationship.

2. Warner, *Generals in Blue*, 293; Ballard, "Grant, McClernand, and Vicksburg," 129–30.

3. Ballard, "Grant, McClernand, and Vicksburg," 138–39; Ballard, *Vicksburg*, 81.

4. Ballard, "Grant, McClernand, and Vicksburg," 139–41; Ballard, *Vicksburg*, 82.

5. Ballard, "Grant, McClernand, and Vicksburg," 143; Winschel, *Triumph & Defeat*, 1:18–19; Terrence J. Winschel, *Triumph & Defeat: The Vicksburg Campaign, Vol. 2* (New York: Savas Beatie, 2006), 2:16.

6. Grant, *Personal Memoirs*, 1:465–66; Edwin C. Bearss, *The Vicksburg Campaign*, vol. 2, *Grant Strikes a Fatal Blow* (Dayton, OH: Morningside House, 1986), 25; Bonekemper, *Grant and Lee*, 215.

7. Grant, *Personal Memoirs*, 1:466; Winschel, *Triumph & Defeat*, 1:25.

8. Grant, *Personal Memoirs*, 1:475–76. The Union gunboats engaged were the *Pittsburg, Louisville, Carondelet, Mound City, Tuscumbia, Lafayette,* and *Benton*. Bearss, *Vicksburg Campaign*, 2:309–13; Winschel, *Triumph & Defeat*, 29–30.

9. Grant, *Personal Memoirs*, 1:477–78; Jason M. Frawley, "'In the Enemy's Country': Port Gibson and the Turning Point of the Vicksburg Campaign," in Woodworth and Grear, *Vicksburg Campaign*, 51; Bearss, *Vicksburg Campaign*, 2:317.

10. Grant, *Personal Memoirs*, 1:477–78; Frawley, "In the Enemy's Country," in Woodworth and Grear, *Vicksburg Campaign*, 51; Bearss, *Vicksburg Campaign*, 2:317.

11. Grant, *Personal Memoirs*, 1:477–78; Frawley, "In the Enemy's Country," in Woodworth and Grear, *Vicksburg Campaign*, 51; Bearss, *Vicksburg Campaign*, 2:317.

12. Grant, *Personal Memoirs*, 1:477–78; Stephen E. Ambrose, *D-Day June 6, 1944: The Climactic Battle of World War II* (New York: Simon and Schuster, 1994), 576; Winschel, *Triumph & Defeat*, 1:30; Bearss, *Vicksburg Campaign*, 2:317; Frawley, "In the Enemy's Country," in Woodworth and Grear, *Vicksburg Campaign*, 51.

13. Grant, *Personal Memoirs*, 1:480–81; Bearss, *Vicksburg Campaign*, 2:318–19; Winschel, *Triumph & Defeat*, 1:57–58.

14. Grant, *Personal Memoirs*, 1:480–81.

15. Winschel, *Triumph & Defeat*, 1:33–34; Bearss, *Vicksburg Campaign*, 2:129–31.

16. *OR*, vol. 24, pt. 3, pp. 45, 50; Timothy B. Smith, *The Real Horse Soldiers: Benjamin Grierson's Epic 1863 Civil War Raid through Mississippi* (El Dorado Hills, CA: Savas Beatie, 2018), 3; Winschel, *Triumph & Defeat*, 1:34, 36–37; Bearss, *Vicksburg Campaign*, 2:129–31; Smith, *Decision Was Always My Own*, 93–94.

17. Smith, *Real Horse Soldiers*, 47–48; Winschel, *Triumph & Defeat*, 1:37.

18. Smith, *Real Horse Soldiers*, 47–48; Winschel, *Triumph & Defeat*,1:37.

19. Smith, *Real Horse Soldiers*, 47–48; Winschel, *Triumph & Defeat*, 1:37.

20. *OR*, vol. 24, pt. 3, p. 95; Winschel, *Triumph & Defeat*, 1:37; Smith, *Real Horse Soldiers*, 50.

21. Winschel, *Triumph & Defeat*, 1:44–55; Smith, *Real Horse Soldiers*, 81, 282. For an interesting in-depth study of Grierson's raid, read Tim Smith's entire book *The Real Horse Soldiers*. The 1959 Hollywood movie *The Horse Soldiers*, starring John Wayne and William Holden, is based loosely on this raid.

22. Ballard, *Vicksburg*, 207; Bearss, *Vicksburg Campaign*, 2:132–76.

23. Ballard, *Vicksburg*, 208–12; Bearss, *Vicksburg Campaign*, 2:254–68; Ballard, *Pemberton*, 139.

24. Grant, *Personal Memoirs*, 1:480–84; Bearss, *Vicksburg Campaign*, 2:407; Ballard, *Vicksburg*, 227–43.

25. Grant, *Personal Memoirs*, 1:491; Hewitt, "Struggle for Port Hudson, Louisiana," 7; Smith, *Decision Was Always My Own*, 113.

26. Warner, *Generals in Blue*, 17–18; McPherson, *Battle Cry of Freedom*, 457–57, 526.

27. *OR*, vol. 24, pt. 3, pp. 181–82; Bearss, *Vicksburg Campaign*, 2:434–35; Ballard, *Vicksburg*, 247–48.

28. *OR*, vol. 24, pt. 3, pp. 181–82; Ballard, *Vicksburg*, 248; Bearss, *Vicksburg Campaign*, 2:431–35.

29. Grant, *Personal Memoirs*, 1:491; *OR*, vol. 24, pt. 3, pp. 181–82; Ballard, *Vicksburg*, 248; Bearss, *Vicksburg Campaign*, 2:431–35.

30. Grant, *Personal Memoirs*, 1:491; *OR*, vol. 24, pt. 3, pp. 181–82; Ballard, *Vicksburg*, 248; Bearss, *Vicksburg Campaign*, 2:431–35.

31. Grant, *Personal Memoirs*, 1:491; *OR*, vol. 24, pt. 3, pp. 181–82; Ballard, *Vicksburg*, 248; Bearss, *Vicksburg Campaign*, 2:431–35.

32. Grant, *Personal Memoirs*, 1:491; *OR*, vol. 24, pt. 3, pp. 181–82; Ballard, *Vicksburg*, 248; Bearss, *Vicksburg Campaign*, 2:431–35.

Chapter 5. Grant's Blitzkrieg

1. Ballard, *Vicksburg*, 257; Winschel, *Triumph & Defeat*, 1:93.

2. Grant, *Personal Memoirs*, 1:491–92; Winschel, *Triumph & Defeat*, 2:13; Smith, *Decision Was Always My Own*, 114; Bearss, *Vicksburg Campaign*, 2:449–52.

3. Grant, *Personal Memoirs*, 1:491–92; Winschel, *Triumph & Defeat*, 2:13; Smith, *Decision Was Always My Own*, 114; Bearss, *Vicksburg Campaign*, 2:449–52.

4. Grant, *Personal Memoirs*, 1:491–92; Winschel, *Triumph & Defeat*, 2:13; Smith, *Decision Was Always My Own*, 114; Bearss, *Vicksburg Campaign*, 2:449–52.

5. Grant, *Personal Memoirs*, 1:491–92; Winschel, *Triumph & Defeat*, 2:13; Smith, *Decision Was Always My Own*, 114; Bearss, *Vicksburg Campaign*, 2:449–52.

6. Grant, *Personal Memoirs*, 1:491–92; Winschel, *Triumph & Defeat*, 2:13; Smith, *Decision Was Always My Own*, 114; Bearss, *Vicksburg Campaign*, 2:449–52.

7. Smith, *Decision Was Always My Own*, 115–25; Winschel, *Triumph & Defeat*, 1:93–94; Winschel, *Triumph & Defeat*, 2:16–17.

8. Author's conjecture.

9. Grant, *Personal Memoirs*, 1:492–93; Winschel, *Triumph & Defeat*, 2:19; Smith, *Decision Was Always My Own*, 118–19.

10. Grant, *Personal Memoirs*, 1:492–93; Winschel, *Triumph & Defeat*, 2:19; Smith, *Decision Was Always My Own*, 118–19.

11. Grant, *Personal Memoirs*, 1:492–93; Winschel, *Triumph & Defeat*, 2:19; Smith, *Decision Was Always My Own*, 118–19.

12. Grant, *Personal Memoirs*, 1:492–93; Winschel, *Triumph & Defeat*, 2:19; Smith, *Decision Was Always My Own*, 118–19.

13. Grant, *Personal Memoirs*, 1:492–93; Winschel, *Triumph & Defeat*, 2:19; Smith, *Decision Was Always My Own*, 118–19.

14. Grant, *Personal Memoirs*, 1:492–93; Winschel, *Triumph & Defeat*, 2:19; Smith, *Decision Was Always My Own*, 118–19.

15. Grant, *Personal Memoirs*, 1:492–93; Winschel, *Triumph & Defeat*, 2:19; Smith, *Decision Was Always My Own*, 118–19.

16. Smith, *Decision Was Always My Own*, 118–19.

17. Author's conjecture.

18. *OR*, vol. 24, pt. 3, pp. 285–86, 297; Smith, *Decision Was Always My Own*, 119–24; Ballard, *Vicksburg*, 257–58.

19. *OR*, vol. 24, pt. 3, pp. 851, 853, 855–56, 860–62; Grant, *Personal Memoirs*, 1:495–97; Ballard, *Vicksburg*, 259–62.

20. Smith, *Decision Was Always My Own*, 124; Ballard, *Vicksburg*, 262–70; William B. Feis, "'Developed by Circumstances': Grant, Intelligence, and the Vicksburg Campaign," in Woodworth and Grear, *Vicksburg Campaign*, 165–66; Winschel, *Triumph & Defeat*, 2:25–28, 165.

21. Smith, *Decision Was Always My Own*, 124; Ballard, *Vicksburg*, 262–70; Feis, "Developed by Circumstances," 165–66; Winschel, *Triumph & Defeat*, 2:25–28, 165.

22. Bearss, *Vicksburg Campaign*, 2:513–14; Smith, *Decision Was Always My Own*, 125–26; Ballard, *Vicksburg*, 271.

23. Bearss, *Vicksburg Campaign*, 2:513–14; Smith, *Decision Was Always My Own*, 125–26; Ballard, *Vicksburg*, 271.

24. Bearss, *Vicksburg Campaign*, 2:513–14; Smith, *Decision Was Always My Own*, 125–26; Ballard, *Vicksburg*, 271.

25. *OR*, vol. 24, pt. 3, pp. 300–301; Grant, *Personal Memoirs*, 1:499–500; Smith, *Decision Was Always My Own*, 125–26; Feis, "Developed by Circumstances," 166–67; Bearss, *Vicksburg Campaign*, 2:513–14.

26. *OR*, vol. 24, pt. 3, pp. 300–301; Ballard, *Vicksburg*, 271; Timothy B. Smith, *Champion Hill: Decisive Battle for Vicksburg* (New York: Savas Beatie, 2006), 89.

27. Grant, *Personal Memoirs*, 1:507; Ballard, *Vicksburg*, 279–80. For additional information on the Battle of Jackson, see Chris Mackowski, *The Battle of Jackson, Mississippi: May 14, 1863* (El Dorado Hills, CA: Savas Beatie, 2022).

28. Ballard, *Vicksburg*, 279.

29. *OR*, vol. 17, pt. 2, pp. 757–58; Woodworth, *Jefferson Davis and His Generals*, 184–85; Craig L. Symonds, "A Fatal Relationship: Davis and Johnston at War," in *Jefferson Davis's Generals*, ed. Gabor S. Boritt (New York: Oxford University Press, 1999), 4.

30. Warner, *Generals in Gray*, 161; Craig L. Symonds, *Joseph E. Johnston: A Civil War Biography* (New York: W. W. Norton, 1992), 10–21; Symonds, "A Fatal Relationship," in Boritt, *Jefferson Davis's Generals*, 8.

31. Gen. Joseph E. Johnston, *Narrative of Military Operations during the Civil War* (1874; repr., New York: Da Capo, 1959), 70–72; Symonds, "A Fatal Relationship," in Boritt, *Jefferson Davis's Generals*, 10; William C. Davis, *Jefferson Davis: The Man and His Hour* (Baton Rouge: Louisiana State University Press, 1991), 356–57; Woodworth, *Jefferson Davis and His Generals*, 176–77.

32. Gen. Joseph E. Johnston, *Narrative of Military Operations during the Civil War*, 70–72; Symonds, "A Fatal Relationship," in Boritt, *Jefferson Davis's Generals*, 10; William C. Davis, *Jefferson Davis: The Man and His Hour* (Baton Rouge: Louisiana State University Press, 1991), 356–57; Woodworth, *Jefferson Davis and His Generals*, 176–77. The five generals nominated by Davis in August 1861 and confirmed by the Confederate Senate were Col. Samuel Cooper, effective May 16; Col. Albert S. Johnston, from May 30; Col. Robert E. Lee, from June 14; Brig. Gen. Joseph E. Johnston, from July 4; and Maj. P. G. T. Beauregard, from July 21. Apparently these appointments were never officially made public. Several historians, including the author, believe that President Davis should have immediately cashiered Johnston for this unnecessary complaining, which might have significantly altered the history of the Civil War.

33. *OR*, vol. 15, p. 820; *OR*, vol. 17, pt. 2, pp. 726–27; Davis, *Jefferson Davis*, 481–85. For ease of identification and simplification the author will refer to the Army of Mississippi and East Louisiana as Pemberton's Command or Army of Vicksburg.

34. Symonds, *Joseph E. Johnston*, 383–85; Symonds, "A Fatal Relationship," in Boritt, *Jefferson Davis's Generals*, 11–12.

35. *OR*, vol. 24, pt. 3, p. 888; Johnston, *Narrative of Military Operations*, 221; Ballard, *Vicksburg*, 274–75, 318.

36. *OR*, vol. 24, pt. 1, p. 215; Johnston, *Narrative of Military Operations*, 222; Ballard, *Vicksburg*, 274–75; Woodworth, *Jefferson Davis and His Generals*, 207.

37. *OR*, vol. 24, pt. 1, p. 215; *OR*, vol. 24, pt. 3, p. 888; Woodworth, *Jefferson Davis and His Generals*, 211; Symonds, *Joseph E. Johnston*, 207–10.

38. *OR*, vol. 24, pt. 1, p. 215; *OR*, vol. 24, pt. 3, p. 888; Woodworth, *Jefferson Davis and His Generals*, 211; Symonds, *Joseph E. Johnston*, 207–10.

39. *OR*, vol. 24, pt. 1, p. 215; *OR*, vol. 24, pt. 3, p. 888; Woodworth, *Jefferson Davis and His Generals*, 211; Symonds, *Joseph E. Johnston*, 207–10.

40. *OR*, vol. 24, pt. 1, p. 215; *OR*, vol. 24, pt. 3, p. 888; Woodworth, *Jefferson Davis and His Generals*, 211; Symonds, *Joseph E. Johnston*, 207–10.

41. *OR*, vol. 24, pt. 1, p. 279; Johnston, *Narrative of Military Operations*, 224–25; Symonds, *Joseph E. Johnston*, 212; Woodworth, *Jefferson Davis and His Generals*, 214, 216; John R. Lundberg, "'I Am Too Late': Joseph E. Johnston and the Vicksburg Campaign," in Woodworth and Grear, *Vicksburg Campaign*, 116–26.

42. *OR*, vol. 24, pt. 1, p. 279; Johnston, *Narrative of Military Operations*, 224–25; Symonds, *Joseph E. Johnston*, 212; Woodworth, *Jefferson Davis and His Generals*, 214, 216; Lundberg, "I Am Too Late," in Woodworth and Grear, *Vicksburg Campaign*, 116–26.

43. Author's conjecture.

44. Winschel, *Triumph & Defeat*, 1:56; Ballard, *Pemberton*, 137–49; Ballard, *Vicksburg*, 203–6, 220.

45. *OR*, vol. 24, pt. 3, p. 842; Ballard, *Pemberton*, 142–43; J. Parker Hills, "Roads to Raymond," in Woodworth and Grear, *Vicksburg Campaign*, 65.

46. Hills, "Roads to Raymond," in Woodworth and Grear, *Vicksburg Campaign*, 74–75; Ballard, *Pemberton*, 142–44.

47. Smith, *Champion Hill*, 135; Smith, *Decision Was Always My Own*, 132–33.

48. *OR*, vol. 24, pt. 3, pp. 876–77; Ballard, *Pemberton*, 153–56; Bearss, *Vicksburg Campaign*, 2:582; Ballard, *Vicksburg*, 282–83.

49. *OR*, vol. 24, pt. 3, pp. 876–77; Ballard, *Pemberton*, 153–56; Bearss, *Vicksburg Campaign*, 2:582; Ballard, *Vicksburg*, 282–83.

50. *OR*, vol. 24, pt. 3, pp. 876–77; Ballard, *Pemberton*, 153–56; Bearss, *Vicksburg Campaign*, 2:582; Ballard, *Vicksburg*, 282–83.

51. *OR*, vol. 24, pt. 3, pp. 876–77; Ballard, *Pemberton*, 153–56; Bearss, *Vicksburg Campaign*, 2:582; Ballard, *Vicksburg*, 282–83.

52. *OR*, vol. 24, pt. 3, p. 877; Ballard, *Vicksburg*, 282–83; Ballard, *Pemberton*, 154–55; Bearss, *Vicksburg Campaign*, 2:568.

53. Ballard, *Vicksburg*, 289–90, 310–11; Winschel, *Triumph & Defeat*, 1:89, 111.

54. Smith, *Champion Hill*, 118–22; Bearss, *Vicksburg Campaign*, 2:574–76.

55. Grant, *Personal Memoirs*, 1:512–13; Smith, *Decision Was Always My Own*, 132–33; Smith, *Champion Hill*, 135. For a detailed account, Timothy Smith's book provides excellent coverage of the Battle of Champion Hill.

56. Smith, *Champion Hill*, 192–222; Winschel, *Triumph & Defeat*, 1:101–3.

57. *OR*, vol. 24, pt. 2, pp. 120–21; Bearss, *Vicksburg Campaign*, 2:607–8; Smith, *Champion Hill*, 234–35; Winschel, *Triumph & Defeat*, 1:104–5.

58. Smith, *Champion Hill*, 239–85; Winschel, *Triumph & Defeat*, 1:105.

59. Smith, *Champion Hill*, 239–85; Winschel, *Triumph & Defeat*, 1:105.

60. Winschel, *Triumph & Defeat*, 1:108–9; Smith, *Champion Hill*, 268–80, 329–37.

61. Winschel, *Triumph & Defeat*, 1:110–11; Smith, *Champion Hill*, 356–61.

62. *OR*, vol. 24, pt. 2, pp. 82, 86, 99, 112, 120; Bearss, *Vicksburg Campaign*, 2:642; Winschel, *Triumph & Defeat*, 1:111–12; Smith, *Champion Hill*, 372.

63. Winschel, *Triumph & Defeat*, 1:112; Ballard, *Pemberton*, 146, 156, 159.

64. Author's conjecture.

Chapter 6. Assaults, Siege, and Surrender

1. *OR*, vol. 24, pt. 1, p. 54; Grant, *Personal Memoirs*, 1:529; Smith, *Decision Was Always My Own*, 153; Timothy B. Smith, *The Union Assaults at Vicksburg: Grant Attacks Pemberton, May 17–22, 1863* (Lawrence: University Press of Kansas, 2020), 69.

2. *OR*, vol. 24, pt. 1, p. 54; Grant, *Personal Memoirs*, 1:529; Smith, *Decision Was Always My Own*, 153; Smith, *Union Assaults at Vicksburg*, 69.

3. *OR*, vol. 24, pt. 1, p. 54; Grant, *Personal Memoirs*, 1:529; Smith, *Decision Was Always My Own*, 153; Smith, *Union Assaults at Vicksburg*, 69; Ballard, *Vicksburg*, 324–25.

4. *OR*, vol. 24, pt. 1, p. 54; Grant, *Personal Memoirs*, 1:529; Smith, *Decision Was Always My Own*, 153; Smith, *Union Assaults at Vicksburg*, 69; Ballard, *Vicksburg*, 324–25.

5. *OR*, vol. 24, pt. 1, p. 54; Grant, *Personal Memoirs*, 1:529; Smith, *Decision Was Always My Own*, 153–54; Winschel, *Triumph & Defeat*, 1:118–19.

6. Smith, *Union Assaults at Vicksburg*, 78–86; Smith, *Decision Was Always My Own*, 154–56.

7. Grant, *Personal Memoirs*, 1:530–31; Smith, *Decision Was Always My Own*, 157–59; Smith, *Union Assaults at Vicksburg*, 145–47.

8. Grant, *Personal Memoirs*, 1:531; Smith, *Union Assaults at Vicksburg*, 153–61; Smith, *Decision Was Always My Own*, 159.

9. Smith, *Decision Was Always My Own*, 160.

10. *OR*, vol. 24, pt. 1, pp. 55–56, 86, 159–65; *OR*, vol. 24, pt. 3, p. 419; Grant, *Personal Memoirs*, 1:531; Smith, *Decision Was Always My Own*, 160–62, 185; Edwin C. Bearss, *The Vicksburg Campaign*, vol. 3, *Unvexed to the Sea* (Dayton, OH: Morningside House, 1986), 836–37, 858–59.

11. Smith, *Union Assaults at Vicksburg*, 61; Bearss, *Vicksburg Campaign*, 3:885.

12. Grant, *Personal Memoirs*, 1:548–49; Smith, *Union Assaults at Vicksburg*, 62–63, 76–77, 414–15, 171; Bearss, *Vicksburg Campaign*, 3:1129–30.

13. Grant, *Personal Memoirs*, 1:574; Smith, *Union Assaults at Vicksburg*, 332–34; Timothy B. Smith, *The Siege of Vicksburg: Climax of the Campaign to Open the Mississippi River, May 23–July 4, 1863* (Lawrence: University Press of Kansas, 2021), 243–49, 454–62.

14. Johnston, *Narrative of Military Operations*, 210–14; Smith, *Siege of Vicksburg*, 337–41.

15. Grant, *Personal Memoirs*, 1:555; Smith, *Decision Was Always My Own*, 191; Smith, *Siege of Vicksburg*, 448.

16. *OR*, vol. 24, pt. 1, pp. 281–83; Ballard, *Pemberton*, 178; Smith, *Siege of Vicksburg*, 406–7, 467–70.

17. *OR*, vol. 24, pt. 1, pp. 281–83; Ballard, *Pemberton*, 178; Smith, *Siege of Vicksburg*, 406–7, 467–70.

18. *OR*, vol. 24, pt. 1, pp. 283–84; Grant, *Personal Memoirs*, 1:556–57; Ballard, *Pemberton*, 178–79, Bearss, *Vicksburg Campaign*, 3:284–85.

19. *OR*, vol. 24, pt. 1, pp. 283–84; Grant, *Personal Memoirs*, 1:556–57; Ballard, *Pemberton*, 178–79, Bearss, *Vicksburg Campaign*, 3:284–85.

20. *OR*, vol. 24, pt. 3, p. 470.

21. *OR*, vol. 24, pt. 3, p. 470; Bearss, *Vicksburg Campaign*, 3:1288–89.

22. *OR*, vol. 24, pt. 3, p. 470; Bearss, *Vicksburg Campaign*, 3:1288–89.

23. Smith, *Decision Was Always My Own*, 198–99; Bearss, *Vicksburg Campaign*, 3:1288.

24. Grant, *Personal Memoirs*, 1:569; Smith, *Decision Was Always My Own*, 198–99.

25. Ballard, *Vicksburg*, 399; Bearss, *Vicksburg Campaign*, 3:1288–89.

26. *OR*, vol. 24, pt. 3, p. 489; Bearss, *Vicksburg Campaign*, 3:1303; Henry S. Commager, ed., *The Blue and Gray: The Story of the Civil War as Told by Participants* (Indianapolis: Bobbs-Merrill, 1950), 2:677.

Chapter 7. Aftermath and Conclusions

1. Ballard, *Vicksburg*, 401–2; Michael R. Bradley, *Decisions of the Tullahoma Campaign: The Twenty-Two Critical Decisions That Defined the Operation* (Knoxville: University of Tennessee Press, 2020), ix–xi, 86.

2. *OR*, vol. 24, pt. 2, p. 325; Grant, *Personal Memoirs*, 1:572; Bearss, *Vicksburg Campaign*, 3:1201, 1311; Ballard, *Vicksburg*, 398–99.

3. The seventeen critical decisions and types are: Davis Appoints Pemberton Commander of the Department of Mississippi and Eastern Louisiana—Personnel; Stanton Appoints Grant to Command the Department of Tennessee—Personnel; Davis Fails to Unify Command of the Mississippi River—Organizational; Grant Decides to Advance South into Mississippi—Operational; Confederates Strike Grant's Supply Line—Tactical; Grant Advances down the West Side of the Mississippi, Bypassing Vicksburg—Operational; Porter Agrees to Run Past Vicksburg—Operational; Grant Decides to Land at Bruinsburg—Tactical; Grierson's Raid and Other Diversions Confuse Pemberton—Operational; Grant Decides Not to Support Banks—Operational; Grant Bypasses Vicksburg and Severs the Confederate Supply Line—Tactical; Grant Limits His Dependence on His Supply Line—Logistical; Grant Strikes at Jackson—Tactical; Johnston Determines He Cannot Assist Pemberton—Operational; Pemberton Mismanages His Defense of Vicksburg—Operational; Grant Assaults the Vicksburg Fortifications—Tactical; Grant Paroles the Confederate Prisoners—Logistical.

4. McPherson, *Battle Cry of Freedom*, 844–45; Ballard, *Vicksburg*, 401–2.

5. Bradley, *Decisions of the Tullahoma Campaign*, xi; McPherson, *Battle Cry of Freedom*, 665.

6. Ballard, *Vicksburg*, 403–4; Ballard, *Pemberton*, 181; Bearss, *Vicksburg Campaign*, 3:1304.

7. Johnston, *Narrative of Military Operations*, 202–10; Ballard, *Vicksburg*, 404–10.

8. Johnston, *Narrative of Military Operations*, 202–10; Ballard, *Vicksburg*, 404–10.

9. Grant, *Personal Memoirs*, 1:579–81; Fuller, *Generalship of Ulysses S. Grant*, 159–60.

10. Grant, *Personal Memoirs*, 2:18-19; McFeely, *Grant: A Biography*, 141-42.

11. Grant, *Personal Memoirs*, 2:32; McPherson, *Battle Cry of Freedom*, 676-77.

12. Grant, *Personal Memoirs*, 1:582–84; 2:32, 64–85; Larry Peterson, *Decisions at Chattanooga: The Nineteen Critical Decisions That Defined the Battle* (Knoxville: University of Tennessee Press, 2018), 67–80.

13. Grant, *Personal Memoirs*, 2:114–15; Larry Peterson, *Decisions of the Atlanta Campaign: The Twenty-One Critical Decisions That Defined the Operation* (Knoxville: University of Tennessee Press, 2019), 16.

14. Grant, *Personal Memoirs*, 2:129–32; McPherson, *Battle Cry of Freedom*, 722.

15. Peterson, *Decisions of the Atlanta Campaign*, 107–8.

16. McPherson, *Battle Cry of Freedom*, 847–50. Surprisingly, Johnston actually commanded and surrendered more men than Lee because of soldiers stationed elsewhere than with his small army.

17. Warner, *Generals in Blue*, 185–86.

18. Warner, *Generals in Blue*, 186.

19. Ballard, *Pemberton*, 184–86, 200; Warner, *Generals in Gray*, 233.

20. Adam Badeau, *Military History of Ulysses S. Grant: From April, 1861, to April, 1865* (New York: D. Appleton, 1881), 1:399–400.

Appendix I. Driving Tour of the Critical Decisions of the Vicksburg Campaign

1. *OR*, vol. 15, p. 820.

2. *OR*, vol. 17, pt. 2, p. 278.

3. *OR*, vol. 24, pt. 3, p. 842.

4. *OR*, vol. 17, pt. 2, p. 297.

5. *OR*, vol. 17, pt. 1, pp. 466–67.

6. Grant, *Personal Memoirs*, 1:422.

7. Grant, *Personal Memoirs*, 1:426–29.

8. *OR*, vol. 17, pt. 1, p. 503.

9. Grant, *Personal Memoirs*, 1:432–33.

10. *OR*, vol. 17, pt. 1, p. 613.

11. Grant, *Personal Memoirs*, 1:442–43.

12. Grant, *Personal Memoirs*, 1:460–61.

13. Grant, *Personal Memoirs*, 1:461.

14. Grant, *Personal Memoirs*, 1:475–76.

15. *OR*, vol. 24, pt. 1, p. 575.

16. *OR*, vol. 24, pt. 1, p. 574.

17. *OR*, vol. 24, pt. 1, p. 48.

18. *OR*, vol. 24, pt. 3, p. 240.

19. *OR*, vol. 24, pt. 3, pp. 242–43.

20. *OR*, vol. 24, pt. 1, p. 48.

21. Grant, *Personal Memoirs*, 1:480–81.

22. *OR*, vol. 24, pt. 1, p. 34.

23. Grant, *Personal Memoirs*, 488–89.

24. *OR*, vol. 24, pt. 1, pp. 49–50.

25. Grant, *Personal Memoirs*, 1:491–92.

26. Grant, *Personal Memoirs*, 1:495.

27. *OR*, vol. 24, pt. 1, p. 50.

28. Grant, *Personal Memoirs*, 1:492–93.

29. *OR*, vol. 24, pt. 1, p. 737.

30. *OR*, vol. 24, pt. 1, pp. 637–38.

31. *OR*, vol. 24, pt. 1, p. 50.

32. Grant, *Personal Memoirs*, 1:499–500.

33. *OR*, vol. 24, pt. 1, p. 50.

34. Grant, *Personal Memoirs*, 1:499–500.

35. *OR*, vol. 24, pt. 1, p. 215.

36. *OR*, vol. 24, pt. 1, p. 215.

37. *OR*, vol. 24, pt. 1, p. 218.

38. *OR*, vol. 24, pt. 1, pp. 222–23.

39. *OR*, vol. 24, pt. 3, p. 870.

40. Grant, *Personal Memoirs*, 1:508–9.

41. *OR*, vol. 24, pt. 1, pp. 52–53.

42. *OR*, vol. 24, pt. 3, p. 859.

43. *OR*, vol. 24, pt. 3, p. 877.

44. *OR*, vol. 24, pt. 3, p. 882.

45. *OR*, vol. 24, pt. 3, p. 884.

46. *OR*, vol. 24, pt. 1, pp. 263–65.

47. *OR*, vol. 24, pt. 3, p. 887.

48. *OR*, vol. 24, pt. 1, p. 241.

49. *OR*, vol. 24, pt. 1, pp. 272–73.

50. *OR*, vol. 24, pt. 3, pp. 326–27.

51. *OR*, vol. 24, pt. 3, p. 329.

52. *OR*, vol. 24, pt. 1, p. 283; Grant, *Personal Memoirs*, 1:556–57.

53. *OR*, vol. 24, pt. 1, pp. 283–84; Grant, *Personal Memoirs*, 1:557–58.

54. *OR*, vol. 24, pt. 1, p. 285; Grant, *Personal Memoirs*, 1:562–63.

55. Grant, *Personal Memoirs*, 1:560–61.

Appendix II. Union Order of Battle

1. Bearss, *Vicksburg Campaign*, 3:957–63; Smith, *Siege of Vicksburg*, 539–51.

Appendix III. Confederate Order of Battle

1. Bearss, *Vicksburg Campaign*, 3:964–68; Smith, *Siege of Vicksburg*, 553–61.

Appendix IV. Reinforcing Vicksburg

1. *OR*, vol. 25, pt. 2, pp. 698–99; Noah A. Trudeau, *Gettysburg: A Testing of Courage* (New York: HarperCollins, 2002), 2–3; Stephen W. Sears, *Gettysburg* (New York: Houghton Mifflin, 2004), 2–3; Palmer, *Lee Moves North*, 43–45.

2. See the preface for more on critical decisions. Matt Spruill, *Decisions at Gettysburg: The Twenty Critical Decisions That Defined the Battle*, 2nd ed. (Knoxville: University of Tennessee Press, 2019), 6–7; Palmer, *Lee Moves North*, 51; Trudeau, *Gettysburg: A Testing of Courage*, 3–4.

3. *OR*, vol. 17, pt. 2, p. 800; Ballard, *Vicksburg*, 14, 87, 121–26, 133–45; Richard M. McMurry, *The Civil Wars of Joseph E. Johnston: Confederate States Army*, vol. 1, *Virginia and Mississippi, 1861–1863* (El Dorado Hills, CA: Savas Beatie, 2023), 192.

4. Ballard, *Vicksburg*, passim. For details of Grierson's raid see Smith, *Real Horse Soldiers*.

5. *OR*, vol. 24, pt. 1, p. 215; McMurry, *Civil Wars of Joseph E. Johnston*, 204–6.

6. *OR*, vol. 25, pt. 2, pp. 724–25; Spruill, *Decisions at Gettysburg*, 9; Sears, *Gettysburg*, 12–13.

7. Ballard, *Vicksburg*, passim; McMurry, *Civil Wars of Joseph E. Johnston*, 235.

8. *OR*, vol. 24, pt. 1, p. 215; McMurry, *Civil Wars of Joseph E. Johnston*, 237–41.

9. Sears, *Gettysburg*, 1; Trudeau, *Gettysburg: A Testing of Courage*, 2, 4.

10. *OR*, vol. 25, pt. 2, pp. 708–9; Palmer, *Lee Moves North*, 51; McMurry, *Civil Wars of Joseph E. Johnston*, 260–62; Trudeau, *Gettysburg: A Testing of Courage*, 4–5; Sears, *Gettysburg*, 14–17.

11. Sears, *Gettysburg*, 498; Trudeau, *Gettysburg: A Testing of Courage*, 529; Winschel, *Triumph & Defeat*, 1:186.

12. Longstreet initially showed interest in going west with his command and therefore would have seemed to be as likely a candidate for the task as anyone. See Gen. James Longstreet, *From Manassas to Appomattox* 1896. Reprint. (New York: Konecky and Konecky, 1992), 435.

13. https:/en. Wikipedia.org, s.v., "List of Established Military Terms," accessed October 2018; McMurry, *Civil Wars of Joseph E. Johnston*, 281–82, 383, 393, 395.

14. Robert C. Black III, *The Railroads of the Confederacy* (Chapel Hill: University of North Carolina Press, 1998), 192–97.

15. John E. Clark, *Railroads in the Civil War: The Impact of Management on Victory and Defeat* (Baton Rouge: Louisiana State University Press, 2001), 80, 94; Ballard, *Vicksburg*, passim.

16. Roger Pickenpaugh, *Rescue by Rail: Troop Transfer and the Civil War in the West, 1863* (Lincoln: University of Nebraska Press, 1998), 28; Black, *The Railroads of the Confederacy* 180–84; Smith, *Siege of Vicksburg*, passim; McMurry, *Civil Wars of Joseph E. Johnston*, 284.

17. Pickenpaugh, *Rescue by Rail*, 28; Black, *The Railroads of the Confederacy* 180–84; Smith, *Siege of Vicksburg*, passim; McMurry, *Civil Wars of Joseph E. Johnston*, 284.

18. Pickenpaugh, *Rescue by Rail*, 28; Black, *Railroads of the Confederacy*, 180–84.

19. McMurry, *Civil Wars of Joseph E. Johnston*, 284; Smith, *Siege of Vicksburg*, 451.

BIBLIOGRAPHY

Primary Sources

Grant, Ulysses S. *Personal Memoirs of U. S. Grant, in Two Volumes.* 2 vols. 1885. Reprint. Harrisburg, PA: Archive Society, 1997.

Johnston, Gen. Joseph E. *Narrative of Military Operations during the Civil War.* 1874. Reprint. New York: Da Capo, 1959.

Longstreet, James. *From Manassas to Appomattox.* 1896. Reprint. New York: Konecky and Konecky, 1992.

Sherman, William T. *Memoirs of General William T. Sherman, by Himself, in Two Volumes.* 2 vols. 1875. Reprint. Harrisburg, PA: Archive Society, 1997.

US War Department. *The War of the Rebellion: A Compilation of the Official Records of the Union and Confederate Armies.* 128 vols. Washington, DC: US Government Printing Office, 1880–1901.

Secondary Sources

Ambrose, Stephen E. *D-Day June 6, 1944: The Climactic Battle of World War II.* New York: Simon and Schuster, 1994.

Badeau, Adam. *Military History of Ulysses S. Grant: From April, 1861, to April, 1865.* 2 vols. New York: D. Appleton, 1881.

Ballard, Michael B. *Pemberton: A Biography*. Jackson: University Press of Mississippi, 1991.

———. *Vicksburg: The Campaign That Opened the Mississippi*. Chapel Hill: University of North Carolina Press, 2004.

Bearss, Edwin C. *The Vicksburg Campaign*. Vol. 1, *Vicksburg Is the Key*. Dayton, OH: Morningside House, 1985.

———. *The Vicksburg Campaign*. Vol. 2, *Grant Strikes a Fatal Blow*. Dayton, OH: Morningside House, 1986.

———. *The Vicksburg Campaign*. Vol. 3, *Unvexed to the Sea*. Dayton, OH: Morningside House, 1986.

Bonekemper, Edward H., III. *Grant and Lee: Victorious American and Vanquished Virginian*. Washington, DC: Regnery, 2012.

Boritt, Gabor S., ed. *Jefferson Davis's Generals*. New York: Oxford University Press, 1999.

Bradley, Michael R. *Decisions of the Tullahoma Campaign: The Twenty-Two Critical Decisions That Defined the Operation*. Knoxville: University of Tennessee Press, 2020.

Buell, Thomas B. *The Warrior Generals: Combat Leadership in the Civil War*. New York: Three Rivers, 1997.

Connelly, Thomas L. *Army of the Heartland: The Army of Tennessee, 1861–1862*. Baton Rouge: Louisiana State University Press, 1967.

Daniel, Larry J. *Days of Glory: The Army of the Cumberland, 1861–1865*. Baton Rouge: Louisiana State University Press, 2004.

Foote, Shelby. *The Civil War, a Narrative: Fort Sumter to Perryville*. New York: Random House, 1958.

Fuller, J. F. C. *The Generalship of Ulysses S. Grant*. 1929. Reprint. New York: Da Capo, 1956.

Hafendorfer, Kenneth A. *Mill Springs: Campaign and Battle of Mill Springs, Kentucky*. Louisville, KY: KH Press, 2010.

Hess, Earl J. *Civil War Infantry Tactics: Training, Combat, and Small-Unit Effectiveness*. Baton Rouge: Louisiana State University Press, 2015.

Hewitt, Lawrence L. "The Struggle for Port Hudson, Louisiana." *Blue & Gray Magazine* 28, no. 1 (2011).

Hughes, Nathaniel C., Jr. *The Battle of Belmont: Grant Strikes South*. Chapel Hill: University of North Carolina Press, 1991.

Jones, Archer. *Civil War Command & Strategy: The Process of Victory and Defeat*. New York: Free Press, 1992.

Jones, R. Steven. *The Right Hand of Command: Use & Disuse of Personal Staffs in the Civil War*. Mechanicsburg, PA: Stackpole Books, 2000.

Joseph, Alvin M. *The Civil War in the American West*. New York: Vintage Books, 1991.

Lewis, Lloyd. *Sherman: Fighting Prophet*. New York: Konecky and Konecky, 1932.

Mackowski, Chris. *The Battle of Jackson, Mississippi: May 14, 1863*. El Dorado Hills, CA: Savas Beatie, 2022.

Marszalek, John E. *Sherman: A Soldier's Passion for Order*. New York: Random House, 1993.

McFeely, William S. *Grant: A Biography*. New York: W. W. Norton, 1981.

McPherson, James M. *Battle Cry of Freedom: The Civil War Era*. New York: Ballantine Books, 1988.

Palmer, Michael A. *Lee Moves North: Robert E. Lee on the Offensive*. New York: John Wiley and Sons, 1998.

Parson, Thomas E. "Thwarting Grant's First Drive on Vicksburg: Van Dorn's Holly Springs Raid." *Blue & Gray Magazine* 17, no. 3 (2010).

Patrick, Jeffrey L. *Campaign for Wilson's Creek: The Fight for Missouri Begins*. Buffalo Gap, TX: McWhiney Foundation Press, 2011.

Peterson, Larry. *Decisions at Chattanooga: The Nineteen Critical Decisions That Defined the Battle*. Knoxville: University of Tennessee Press, 2018.

———. *Decisions of the 1862 Kentucky Campaign: The Twenty-Seven Critical Decisions That Defined the Operation*. Knoxville: University of Tennessee Press, 2019.

———. *Decisions of the Atlanta Campaign: The Twenty-One Critical Decisions That Defined the Operation*. Knoxville: University of Tennessee Press, 2019.

Smith, Timothy B. *Champion Hill: Decisive Battle for Vicksburg*. New York: Savas Beatie, 2006.

———. *The Decision Was Always My Own: Ulysses S. Grant and the Vicksburg Campaign*. Carbondale: Southern Illinois University Press, 2018.

———. *Grant Invades Tennessee: The 1862 Battles for Forts Henry and Donelson*. Lawrence: University Press of Kansas, 2016.

———. *The Real Horse Soldiers: Benjamin Grierson's Epic 1863 Civil War Raid through Mississippi.* El Dorado Hills, CA: Savas Beatie, 2018.

———. *Shiloh: Conquer or Perish.* Lawrence: University Press of Kansas, 2014.

———. *The Siege of Vicksburg: Climax of the Campaign to Open the Mississippi River, May 23–July 4, 1863.* Lawrence: University of Press of Kansas, 2021.

———. *The Union Assaults at Vicksburg: Grant Attacks Pemberton, May 17–22, 1863.* Lawrence: University Press of Kansas, 2020.

Symonds, Craig L. *Joseph E. Johnston: A Civil War Biography.* New York: W. W. Norton, 1992.

Warner, Ezra J. *Generals in Blue: Lives of the Union Commanders.* Baton Rouge: Louisiana State University Press, 1964.

———. *Generals in Gray: Lives of the Confederate Commanders.* Baton Rouge: Louisiana State University Press, 1959.

Winschel, Terrence J. *Triumph & Defeat: The Vicksburg Campaign.* Vol. 1. New York: Savas Beatie, 2004.

———. *Triumph & Defeat: The Vicksburg Campaign.* Vol. 2. New York: Savas Beatie, 2006.

———. *Chickasaw Bayou: Sherman's Winter of Despair. Blue & Gray Magazine* 26, no. 3 (2009).

Woodworth, Steven E. *Jefferson Davis and His Generals: The Failure of Confederate Command in the West.* Lawrence: University Press of Kansas, 1990.

Woodworth, Steven E., and Charles D. Grear, eds. *The Vicksburg Campaign: March 29–May 18, 1863.* Carbondale: Southern Illinois University Press, 2013.

INDEX

Numbers in **boldface** refer to illustrations